T0193910

The *Wound's* Been Found

JENNIFER MOQUIN

WESTBOW
PRESS®
A DIVISION OF THOMAS NELSON
& ZONDERVAN

To Contact Author:

jennifermoquin.org

P.O. Box 2267
Sarasota, Florida 34238

WestBow Press books may be ordered through booksellers or by contacting:

WestBow Press
A Division of Thomas Nelson & Zondervan
1663 Liberty Drive
Bloomington, IN 47403
www.westbowpress.com
1 (866) 928-1240

ISBN: 978-1-5127-7984-4 (sc)
ISBN: 978-1-5127-7985-1 (hc)
ISBN: 978-1-5127-7983-7 (e)

Library of Congress Control Number: 2017904151

Print information available on the last page.

WestBow Press rev. date: 12/21/2018

To my children. You will always be my kids. May each of you capture your own dream and live out the legacy, knowing Christ and exactly who you are in Him, remembering not to ever settle. The best is yet to come.

Onward Christian soldiers! To God be the glory!

In loving memory of *my Papa*! I made it … and I am more than okay!

Under His Wings

Most everyone that I know have seen the movie *The Karate Kid*. Daniel-san started to prepare for his dream. The preparation that he needed did not start off the way that he had imagined. Not even close. Wax on, wax off. Over and over again. The cute little old man would have him do it again! Over and over again. And Daniel-san did not look very happy about it to begin with either. He was rather frustrated, and he didn't understand his teacher's instruction. It did not make sense to his mind whatsoever. But he did choose to hang in there and to obey the instruction. It would pay off in the long run.

I have not always understood my instructor either—even when God first led me to write this book. My first thought was, *No way! I do not know how.* Writing nice letters was one thing, but an entire book was another. I did not even have great computer skills. Actually, the little bit that I did have had been long forgotten. For me, it was a challenge—a challenge that turned into quite the fight. I am not afraid of challenging situations. I have not always liked them or enjoyed them. But this was a different story altogether.

I have been told many times from different people that I would have made a great lawyer. I laugh inside about it because it is probably true. I do have that fight and feistiness inside of me. I have been known to be very argumentative and opinionated. But I have not had the patience for debating. It was a complete turn off to me. When I knew what was true and what I believed in, then that was it for me. You were not going to change my mind about it. When I set my mind to something, I am determined to see it happen.

It is all about desire. And when my heart gets wrapped up around that desire, I am not going to back down. In fact, I am no quitter. I'm not saying that I do not wear out and grow weary and tired because those times and seasons have definitely come. But it is a choice whether or not one remains there. I have chosen to get back up and to get going. There she goes—she rides again! That is how I now see myself. There is no satisfaction in giving up.

It is a choice to press on to the goal—to the dream. I never in my wildest dreams realized the great opposition that would come against me—that is, until it all happened. I started out my new journey by experience. I did not have classroom time that taught me what I needed to know. Nor did I have the real truth from the greatest book that was ever written. I got to learn the hard way. But those experiences came in ways that I would have never gotten sitting inside some classroom.

I did not like school growing up. I would bore very easily, many times falling asleep in class. My interest was just not there. I had a mind of my own … and a wild imagination. I was a dreamer, and I was ridiculed for being one too. But it did not stop me. It caused me to second-guess myself. And that right there has caused me more trouble and pain then I could ever describe. It has been one of my worst enemies. It is one thing to be rejected by others and people you love, and it is another thing to be rejected by your own self.

The dreaming inside of me would not leave me alone. I tried to stop it. I tried to push and shove it out of my way. It did not work. It was still there. A constant companion. A dream.

Your enemy will use other people to try to make you think that you're crazy, that dreams do not come true, that it's all fantasy land. Your enemy will tell you to wake up and get into the real world. I am here to tell you that I have been awakened and that my eyes have been opened wide to the real truth. And I have my own experiences to go all along with it. Dreams are real. And dreams do come true. I have my own Cinderella story, and it's one that I have been instructed to tell. It is one worth telling after all. It is one that people will want to hear. I am sure of it. For some, it may be their worst nightmare. But for others, it can be a real-life story to bring hope—hope for a much brighter future, hope for today and a better tomorrow. One thing is for sure. "This too shall pass." Nothing stays the same forever. Things change, and they will change for the better if you are persistent in your expectations and in your belief system. You just have to make up your mind that you are not going to give up and that you are in for the long haul no matter how long it takes. I have lost at little battles, but I have won the war.

I heard it said that sometimes you have to lose your mind in order to find it. That is what happened to me, and I am so glad that it did. My mind, the way that I once thought, got me into too much trouble. It brought about evil and undesirable circumstances. You know, where the mind goes, the man or woman follows. And I never want to go back there. That was a dark and lonely place. You can have people all around you and yet be the loneliest person alive. People will not fulfill you. And people will not make you happy. Happiness is a choice. And sometimes you have to get totally away from certain people to find your truth, to discover your own happiness, and to discover what it really means to be fulfilled. And when you do decide to move forward and get out from the pit you have been living in, do not be surprised if those people try to stop you. Some people can be our worst enemies. And they can even be family members. *Selah!* Pause and think of that.

There are all sorts of people in this world who give themselves titles. Some have earned it, while others just take it on. Not everyone is who they claim to be—even those who call themselves Christians. It is so very easy to talk the talk, but then it is another thing entirely to walk the walk. There are many talkers in this world. We need more doers. And so many of those talkers sit back and judge the doers. It is all about choice. Some are willing to be led in the right direction. Some are willing to hang out with their instructor God long enough to be instructed. Some will never even get started. They will just spend their lives talking about what could be and what should be but never doing what is necessary to get the results that they really desire.

I refuse to be one of those people. I am not going to one day turn into some granny sitting in my rocking chair, an old woman with long gray hair, complaining about what could have been. That would be living my entire life in a ball of regret. That is not me. I like adventure. I am a risk-taker. I do take risks—some big and others smaller. It does not really matter. A risk is a risk. Even when everything is on the line and even if you win some and lose other times, you are never a loser unless you quit. I do not want to die sitting inside a box of complete boredom.

My husband, Larry, enjoys watching boxing on television from time to time. He is not much of the sports fan. But he has always liked his boxing. One thing that I do love about him is that he would—and will—always choose me over any boxing match. That was one specific thing that I had requested—that if I ever got to live in my new life with a new husband, then please do not give me one who is a sports fanatic. There is nothing wrong with sports, and I was once a cheerleader. Eventually, I even learned some things about the game of football. I did relish in the enjoyment and excitement of a touchdown. It was quite the thrill. I just wanted a man who would recognize me regardless of what was going on. I no longer wanted to waste away, sitting on some sort of sideline. I wanted to be inside of the game. I wanted to be a real live player in the middle of the action. I wanted my own sport. I wanted my own game to play out. I was bored of trying to sit back on the sofa and watch others play out theirs. I wanted and desired my own. I no longer wanted to ride in the backseat of this life. There was too much inside of me to sit there another moment and watch life pass me by. I had my very own touchdown to make. Little did I know that once I got my ball in hand and decided to run with it, a world full of people would be after me—and not because they wanted to go where I was going. They wanted to stop me and to knock me down. There are dream thieves out there. Some are much closer to you than you may think, and not all are who they claim to be. You will have your Judas moment. Betrayed by a kiss! It will break your heart too. I know all about it. It's happened more times than once.

The dream is what kept me alive in some of my darkest hours and seasons. It gave me an ounce of hope for what could be or what could come. The what-if factor was operative in me. I dreamed of having a man who would really love me, one who would treat me right and adore me. I wanted that, even though I was made to believe that I did not deserve it. No person can make you believe anything that you do not already believe yourself. They cannot just take over your mind and your heart unless you give them access. It is easy to believe the lies some people have told us when we do not know the truth for our own self. Childhood can sting many of us, leaving its trail of damage into our adult years. One situation to the next. One cycle of dysfunction to another. That's not a pleasant world to live in. You may always wonder, *What in the world is wrong?* Or worse, *what in the world is wrong with me?* Have you ever asked yourself that question? That is what played over and over inside of my head like a broken recorder. *What is wrong with you? What did Jennifer go and do now?* It went all the way back to childhood. Jennifer this, and Jennifer that. She must be the one to blame.

Lies, lies, lies, and more lies. Where was her truth. Why did not anyone step up and help her? Perhaps the fear of being found out. Shame, I suppose, was at play. Jennifer knew all about shame. She lived that old life of hers in a constant shame-based persona. She was ashamed of where she came from, who she came from. She did not like the insecurities that she monitored and wanted no part in being that way. She judged harshly and had no clue about the door she had opened up for herself. Her life was not her dream. It did not even start off in the right way.

Where was her Mr. Right, her knight in shining armor? Was he even out there for her? She questioned time and time again. She hoped. That's all she had—a tiny seed of hope. Everything else had been stripped away. Jennifer wanted security. She wanted to feel safe. Her life was a mess. She did not even consider it a life. She felt so alone, and she was stuck in such a deep, dark pit. She questioned over and over how she had gotten there to begin with. How did such disaster happen to her? What had she ever done to deserve what she had been served? Have any of those thoughts ever tormented you over and over again? It is torture when you do not know the answers to your problems. Everything around you and inside of you feels so very wrong. You think that you are the problem and that everything you do, think, and feel is wrong. There is nothing right about you, and you question why you are even here. Why were you ever born into this world in the first place? You think that you were an accident. Jennifer did. That was what she thought over and over again until she was twenty-four years old. Then something happened to Jennifer that would change her course. It would change the direction of her life.

Too many times to count, she wanted to be out from this place. Or so she thought. She wanted to just die and end the madness inside and out, to get away from her enemy, the one who was constantly attacking her. She had been beat up to her very core. The pain had gotten to her heart. Bruises on the skin will eventually heal. They go away, and the skin goes back to its original color. At least hers did. But the heart is a different matter altogether. It is not even like a scab that has bled. It is a very tender yet profound organ. I don't think that everything that goes on in the heart can really be put into exact words. People ridiculing and making fun of you for being so shallow is not pleasant. Those were Jennifer's teenage years. They were miserable. And she covered it all up with a pretty face and awesome hair. I think she had great hair. Not all have hair like that. It was a nice gift. Jennifer did not have very much to offer. But she was willing to give what she did have. I think of her as a lifetime giver. She has always been a giver, and for her, once a giver, always a giver. But new requirements in her giving would come. She would not stay the same.

How she viewed herself as a child turned into how she viewed herself as a teen. Then the teen went into her adulthood, still living with the same old views and the same old lies. But she did not recognize them as lies. They had been her truth. They were taught at a young age. Jennifer grew up believing something that was just not true. It was true to her, but it wasn't the real truth. It is amazing how we attract those others who will just feed our fears—same old cycle, same old merry-go-rounds. And around and around she had gone too many times. And she had had enough.

So there she was lying flat on her face on a cold bathroom floor, crying. Yes, Jennifer cried. But it was behind closed doors where no one would see. She was a warrior. She was the so-called "tough cookie." She was not going to break. She was not allowed to break. That went against the rules in her head. Jennifer hated weakness, and she did not tolerate being around weak people very well. They got on her nerves. She did not have much compassion for others in pain. Her heart attitude was to buck up and bear it. *Get your act together, and stop your whining.* She would think to herself, *If you only knew what I have been through, you would have no reason to complain.* It is true. She was just being real.

Jennifer was hard-hearted. She had to be. That was the only way she knew how to deal with her life. And she was not ready to bring the deep issues of her heart out into the open seas of life. At least not yet. She had only just begun preparing for this process.

Jennifer cried out to the God she had been taught about. She believed in Him just fine. She even believed in Jesus as her Savior. She got that part. She believe that God existed, but she didn't believe that He would love her or be good to her. All of her materialism came from her papa. He played daddy to Jennifer. He was her role model. He was the one her heart wanted to please. He had rescued her time and time again, starting from when she was just five years of age. He came in times when it seemed like her entire little world fell apart.

Jennifer had been taught and brought up in religion. She knew all about the do's and the don'ts. If you do this, then you go to hell. You'd better choose Jesus so that you don't go to hell. It was such a scary way to try to receive salvation. And she had never been taught about the receiving part anyway, not in any sort of way that she could remember. It was all about doing or not doing—doing this and doing that, giving this and giving that. She had been taught all sorts of Scripture passages, but in a twisted form. It was not the real, true nature of God. But really, people cannot teach the real God and His real nature if they do not know Him for themselves. I mean, you cannot give away something that you do not have. You must have it first in order to really give it. And let me say that God, the God that I have come to know personally for my own self, is not a thing. He is a living Spirit.

There she lay, crying out to Him. Would He answer? Jennifer did not want to live another day the way she had been living. It was not a life that she felt was worth living. She had pleaded with her God plenty of times before to take her out from this place. There were so many nights of despair year after year. She didn't want to go through another day, another night. There was one season that was so bad for her that the only thing that kept her from taking her own life was something that a person had once told her, "If you take your life, then you go to hell, for it is not yours to take." That was stuck in her brain. She was too scared to see if it was true or not. So instead she would pray and ask God to just come and take her out from her misery. And He did not do it. Nor did He allow something else to take her life. She had been praying in faith that her prayer would be heard and answered. She prayed so many nights could be the last. It sure felt like the end was coming too. It was a constant battle. It scared Jennifer, for she did not know how to fight that battle. It was a very dangerous situation. There was no doubt about that. It was so embarrassing and humiliating to make 911 calls every evening in the midnight hours. It seemed like the entire police force got to know her. That was not the life that she had dreamed of as a little girl. Some had warned her, but she chose this life anyhow. Papa did not approve of the relationship, but he allowed it. Jennifer was not going to take no for an answer. I have gone through too many situations with my own children now to understand. There are times when a person just won't listen to your heart or your instructions. Nor will some people respect your authority. They just won't listen to you, period. Sometimes you just have to say, "Well, have at it!" It hurts when you know the path they are on and where it leads. So you pray. You pray and keep on praying and confessing and predicting that child's life. You do not speak out death and what they are doing. But you speak life. You call it in. You call in by speaking out what you want to see, what God's will is. You stay in faith. You fight the good fight of faith regardless of what is taking place. It will pay off. Even if it gets way worse before it gets better.

Jennifer would pack up all of her belongings, including all of her shoes. And she had so many shoes too. Then before the next day was up, she would move right back in. She did not want to be treated the way she had been treated. She wanted to believe that it would get better and the abuse would stop. It only went from bad to worse. Then it went from worse to whatever would be considered worse than worse. Jennifer could not change another person. People do not change people. God changes people. And He only changes people who want to be changed. God gives man and woman free will to choose. God does not force Himself onto a human being. He is a real gentleman. He must be wanted and invited. He gets blamed for things that are not His fault.

Jennifer obviously is not the same person today as she was then. The Jennifer I have come to know would not be attracted to that type and would not have tolerated the behavior evident on the first date. Jennifer did not see herself accurately and truthfully. She didn't know to her true identity. She didn't know who she really was then or who she really belonged to. Jennifer had no clue about who she was. She existed, and she wanted to know why.

Even though her papa did not like or approve of some of the things Jennifer chose and got herself into, he still did not turn his back on her. He was there through it all. Through thick and thin, he was there. Jennifer knew that she could always go to him and he would help, even if it was just for encouragement. It was not always about him giving his money to her or bailing her out of credit card debt. He was way more to her than that. In Jennifer's eyes, her papa was her hero. Money could not fix what needed to be fixed inside of Jennifer's heart. Money would not fill the void. All of the shopping was fun and quite nice, but it did not heal her. It did not fix her. It did not remove the wounds.

Jennifer was at a point where she wanted to know if God would be good to her, if God would actually love somebody like herself. She had grown to the point of feeling unlovable. That is what abuse and neglect and lots of lies will do to a person. Would He? This God that she believed in revealed Himself to her that very night on the cold bathroom floor. Regardless of all that Jennifer had done wrong and the rules that she had broken, He showed up anyway. Jennifer could not comprehend it. It went against all of the teachings in her head. She thought He loved the perfect ones, those who did all the so-called right things, those who behaved right, those who talked just right, those who sat in the church pews Sunday after Sunday, those who looked right, those who walked in love. Jennifer's idea of what love looked like was very distorted. Jennifer had no idea of what real, genuine, unconditional love looked like. Not even her papa could give her that. She was clueless. Jennifer thought she loved others, and she loved the only way that she knew how. But it was out from a heart full of fear. It was nothing close to a perfect kind of love.

Who was this God Jennifer had heard of and believed in? He came to her by His Spirit in a way that she had not experienced before. He is so very compassionate and understanding and loving. She had not known those traits about Him. He was so merciful to her. Jennifer did not even know what having mercy was. She had the yard-stick mentality of God. She had viewed God having a ruler out, slamming it at her, not happy with what she had done, not happy with her. Many things had gone all wrong in her life. Some of those choices and decisions she made were so wrong. But God stepped into the scene of her life as she was lying there alone on the bathroom floor. She was serious in her desperation to find Him. She wanted Him to come to come to her rescue. Jennifer could not take anymore. Not another round. Not another minute or second. She was desperate for Him. Jennifer wanted out, but this time not in death. She already felt so dead anyway. She was still breathing, and her heart was still beating. She wanted an escape route. It felt like fires were burning rapidly all around her. The flames were intensifying and closing in on her. It was get out or die. The light got turned on for her so that she could now see. Grace stepped in. And she did get back up. Jennifer was no longer being forced to stay down. She arose! She got out, and she went free.

What I came to realize is this: I did not know God at all. I was taught Him. I was taught rules and regulations, many of which I had violated. I was taught all sorts of things in the religious world. But I was not taught the true, living, breathing Lord. He was nothing that I thought He was. And I realized that I no longer had to run away from Him when I messed up and missed the mark. He actually drew me closer to Him. He wanted me. He wanted me to run to Him, to run into His arms. The opportunity that He gives us is so very awesome. He is loving. He is a loving Father. What He does for one, He will do for another. God does not play favorites, even though He makes me feel like I am His very favorite one. He makes me feel so close and so very special to Him. He can do the same for you.

The pain of the journey has been well worth it. And I know the best is yet to come. It should be getting better and better, brighter and brighter, lighter and lighter! Jennifer came to the point of wanting to know Him. God got her out from some real messes. There was a wait time involved in the majority of them. And it wasn't so pleasant either. Jennifer did not yet know or understand what it meant to say that the joy of the Lord is her strength or to allow His peace to surpass all of her understanding. That would have been foreign to her head. And her heart still was in major need of a healing. It still bled.

Jennifer was beginning to realize that God was actually very interested in her. She liked that. It made her smile for real—no faking about it. She began trusting Him in financial areas. God gave her things that she once could have only dreamed of. Like the high-end bag, for instance. God had Jennifer's attention. He was showing her that she could trust Him. He was not trying to push Himself onto her. That is not how He operates. The Devil pushes and shoves while God leads and guides. God did not have a horse whip out after all.

Papa and Jennifer had a relationship. He did things for her. He would even sit on the bench at the mall and let her shop. He did not complain if she took awhile either. He would just smile. She was glad that she was having fun. And Jennifer always liked their trips to Disney World. Jennifer took the time to know her papa. She listened to his very long lectures as respectfully as she could. She would give a fake laugh at his jokes. I do not remember her having very much sense of humor then. She tried. Papa had a way of getting her to smile time and time again. He was always trying to see her smile. Papa saw the sadness that Jennifer carried around. He would tell her how good-looking she was. He would tell her how special she was to him. He was a good father to her. He was flawed, but he loved her. Papa was her stability. She always knew where she stood with him. There was no roller-coaster ride with him. He was consistent all the way to the very end.

Sitting in church all those years time and time again was not enough for Jennifer. Giving to those in need was not enough. Tithing was not enough. Giving over and above was not enough. The American dream was not enough. The nice, large, fully decorated home was not enough. Her upscale car was not enough. The wardrobe she once could only dream of was not enough. The name-brand shoes were not enough. Her high-end bag was not enough. Jennifer's life was full of material things, nice things. It wasn't that she got every little (or large) thing every time she wanted it. She did remember her children, and she observed that when she made up her mind and believed something, she eventually got what she said that she would get. (That thought helps me now remember that about myself.)

She lived a very blessed life. She was a stay-at-home mom with a business of her own. Jennifer had her own checking account, and no one was breathing down her neck and ridiculing her about how she spent her money. She was a free woman—at least in some areas anyway. Jennifer was on her road to real freedom.

Jennifer had been given a devotional book years ago and was diligent in her reading. Every morning before she would leave the house, she had her quiet time for prayer and reading. She reviewed one short page a day. It brought encouragement to her in her Christian walk. As far as actual Bible reading and study time went, she was not a fan. The few times she dared to open up her Bible, it spoke condemnation to her. Jennifer was in need of a brain transplant and a new heart surgery. She needed both. It is far easier for a nonbeliever to hear the real truth and receive it and accept it than it is for a person to grow up with a religious, law-abiding doctrine and then have to relearn everything the right way. It's not an easy program, but that was the task I had been assigned. I ran for so long in doubt. I just could not run away from that inner calling anymore. I was tired and bored and felt worn out. I somehow knew that I was missing something, something that I had not even begun to understand. So back to school Jennifer went, but not in an actual classroom environment. However, she was enrolled in school and in a training program at the school of the Holy Ghost. Read on, and I pray for you to really see.

It amazes me how many do-overs that I have actually had in the writing of this book. I honestly do not know the number of times. I have lost count. Each manuscript keeps getting shorter. The girl who was once so quiet and shallow who did not want people knowing her life turned into one who would go and tell all! I'm not kidding! Once I got that truth inside of me and the lights got turned on, I was telling everyone. And I did. I would tell anyone who was willing to sit and to listen to it all. Just about all the details came spilling right out of my mouth. I didn't hold much of anything back. I had gone from one extreme to another. I had found my voice and was no longer afraid to go out and use it. That was another lesson.

Each time the do-over comes, I come to like it even more. I think, *Oh, wow, this one is so much better.* In fact, I would not even want people to read some of the other things that I wrote. It would not even be appropriate. But that is not how I saw it in the beginning. I wanted to tell it all. I would have been glad to give out very specific details. I was hurting very badly, still feeling damaged. I needed to lash out. I had my own horse whip in hand—if you get what I mean. I would have been so very glad to use it too.

I have my own instructor. He is far better than any gym trainer I've ever known. I did not like the results I ended up with. I did not want bulk but lean muscle. It is sort of like the writing of this book—not so much bulk but leanness. Anyhow, my instructor knows what He is doing far better than I know myself. He is my very own personal trainer. And I get along with Him quite well. I am not near as bossy with God. I used to tell that gym trainer, "No way! I am not doing that exercise. It hurts my knees, and that one messes up my freshly pedicured toenails!" I am thankful that I did get the time and money to have a trainer of my own. It was an experience.

I now prefer my kind of exercise, the ones I can do in the privacy of my own home. I have come to live as a pretty reserved person. Working those faith muscles has become my thing. I have found my sport. I am becoming a very well-trained athlete. I have my own game to play after all.

It would be so disappointing to waste it. How can one help anyone or be any real value to another person in need if you are not willing to be genuine? For me, I needed some details. In order for me to begin this journey, I needed someone who was not afraid to stand up and share his or her own personal journey. I needed some details to encourage me. Or I would not have gotten up from where I was. I was once so naive. I once thought that a preacher or minister would be perfect, someone who didn't break the rules in order for God to use him or her. I did not know better. I did not know that all had sinned and needed forgiveness. I had not been taught that. I guess that somewhere in my old thinking, I really thought that there were some perfect people walking around on this earth. Okay, there are some perfect people living here today, but only because of Jesus and all that He has done for us, for you and me. Once one receives Him, then He makes you perfect. But one is not perfect from abiding by some law or a set of rules and regulations. That is religion and has nothing to do with Jesus and why Jesus came to earth. I am telling you the truth when I say that I needed a brain transplant. I needed an entire mind renewal. I was so off and so very clueless about what the truth looked like.

I did not think that people who stood behind a pulpit experienced some of the things that the old me had done. I just did not think it was possible. So the lie inside of my head played on, "Who do you think you are? How in the world do you think God could use someone like you?" Oh, yeah. It went on and on and on until I was able to rise up and shut that voice down. I did not know who I was, so how was I supposed to answer that tormenting question that played itself against me? I did not have an answer. Who are you? Do you know? It was not about me being Jennifer Moquin and being a wife and a mother and a business owner and so forth. All of that was a blessing, but it had nothing to do with who I was. Who was I? I was determined to find out. I yearned for the discovery of my own identity. I wanted to get free to be me—whoever that was. It was time to go a little deeper. It was a step-by-step program I found myself called to. It was up to me to keep going. How far are you willing to go? I wanted to go all the way through. I wanted to come alive like I had never lived before. I did not just want to go through motions day after day. I had an excitement for life that I was able to express when I met Larry. And he caught it little by little. He was a heathen when I first met him, but he did not stay that way. My faith was contagious, and he caught what I had!

There was so much more to be discovered. Nothing was going to stop me. Desire was in action. "There she goes! We must do something to stop her! She is getting away! Oh no! We will have to report this to the boss," one says. "And that is not something that I want to do. We must do all we can do to stop this woman in going a step further." Just imagine it for a moment—one getting freer and freer from the enemy at play. This enemy does not play fair. Nor does he fight fair. One must learn his tactics in order to play the game, to stay in the game and to win the game. Touchdown! I am going for the goal. No matter how many times I get tackled and knocked down. I have made up my mind in advance to get back up and to keep running in the game, to keep running the race set before me. I have been given my own football, ladies and gentlemen. I was told to hold on to it with my life. My ball symbolizes my dream—the dream that God gave to me. The enemy is a dream thief, a dream killer. But he never managed to kill it for good. He has tried to put the light out of my fire. But the fire comes right back to life. Then the enemy tries again with another set of circumstances. He tries to blow it out for good. I truly believe that that Devil thought plenty of times that he had gotten me for good. Not so. I am still here! I did get back up, even though he had me as far down as one could get. I know all about that situation. I did not read about it. I lived it. What is he the enemy going to do with a person who just will not quit, one who will not tolerate his lies, one who will search out the truth and not just believe any old thing taught by a granny or a teacher?

I mean, what can the enemy really do to a person who is just going to keep going forward regardless of what he brings? He can keep trying to be a pest. Once you really know who you are and understand who he is, it will change your life. He uses a great deal of fear to try to stop or to come against a person. But what can this enemy do to one who no longer fears him? What can he do when that person knows that he or she has been given power over him and all that he tries to do. The enemy then is the one who is really scared. He never wanted you to get to that mind-set in the first place. That is why he has worked so hard to keep you from knowing and understanding who you really are and the power that is inside of you. Once you have been born again, you receive Jesus as your Savior, and He takes all of your past and all of your sins and gives you all of Him. He becomes yours, and you are His. It is a gift. There is no such thing as one trying to earn it. You cannot work your way into heaven. No one is ever good enough or perfect enough. Only Jesus is perfect. Some people out there make it more complicated than what it really is. I have very much enjoyed my new life, my new birth in Christ Jesus. Oh, it has been worth it. I would be dead without Him. I had no life without Him in it. I enjoy my new identity. I am enjoying this life to the very fullest. I am determined to enjoy this life, my life. I have one life to live. There is no such thing as coming back as somebody else or as a butterfly. You have one life to live, and I encourage you to live it … and to live it well.

I am now quite pleased with my existence and where I come from. I come from God. I got born again and belong to Him. I am His child. And when your mother and your father have forsaken you, God will adopt you as His very own. I like that even better. I like having Him as my own parent. It just took what seemed like a lifetime for me to receive the truth. I am so very thankful for the opportunity of a new birth and a fresh life to start with Him after I was reborn. Receiving Jesus as your

Savior is so much more than just using Him as a fire escape so that you don't end up in hell. God knows the heart of a man or woman. He knows why we do certain things and why we don't. Nobody is going to fool God. And I do mean no one. Regardless of how smart you think you are, God is smarter.

I am also so very thankful when the truth prevails in the life of a believing Christian. All that was hidden and covered up will come out into the marvelous light, and once it has been exposed, then you can deal with it once and for all. Then it no longer has power over you. That was what Jennifer was after. She wanted her truth. But she needed it as well. She would not ever go totally free without it. She would live in a continual cycle of torment until it was discovered. In fact, it would open up her eyes to the reason she had thought the way she had thought, felt the way she had felt, and acted out the way she once acted. It would explain the struggles of her life. It would explain the pain behind the surface—pain she had buried so deep, hoping to forget it. It is almost like being buried alive. You are alive, breathing and taking in air, but you feel so weighed down. It's so much weight for one to carry. The load of it is just too heavy. It's unbearable. It is so bad that your mind tries to tell you that the incident never happened. You did not get the help that you needed, so you even try telling yourself that it just never happened. You live a lie. You thought you covered it up by forgetting about it. But inside, it eats away at you day after day. It festers and causes you to act out in ways that you do not like or understand. You wish you would live differently, but you don't know how to get there. You try to love the only way that you know how. But it is just not good enough. Nothing that you do ever seems to be good enough. Perfectionism when at play will eventually wear you out. *Maybe if I do this, then this person will love me. Or if I do that, then I will be accepted.* On and on it will go. It is called "people pleasing." That was my addiction. I was addicted to people's approval. It was nothing but a life of misery—one disappointment after another, one hurt after another, one letdown to another. I had a heart that was desperate to please.

I stood there that very day in a department store that had become very familiar to me. I had plenty of money to spend. But then suddenly after arriving there, I realized that there was no longer anything there for me. Sure, I could have found some cute things. But the desire and interest for those things had temporarily left me. I just felt an emptiness and a longing for God that I had not felt before. I wanted more. I stood there like a starving person. Those short little daily devotions were no longer working for me. It was not enough. Going to church was not cutting it for me either. Anyone can show up and sit there. I was not even in the right place. I knew it. But had no idea where my right place was. I had no idea whatsoever of the location. All I knew was that I needed a desperate change. I was the real desperate housewife. There was no acting involved. This was serious.

I stood there thinking to myself, *If I died today, do I really even know my maker? Do I know Him?* I would stand before Him, and He would be a stranger to me. Remember, I knew what He could do for me in the financial department. I had released my faith for many great things and had gotten them from Him. I also knew about how He had fought a really big battle for me and how He had won. (I will get into that later.) There was more to His person that I wanted to know. I was not just curious but hungry for Him. Like really hungry for the things of God. It was just in me to want to know … for myself. I was fed up with trying to live from another's faith. That did not work out right. I had my own faith, and I desired to live it out myself without another person trying to be the god in my life. Many people did not just get up and walk away either. Nor did they want to stop talking and trying to tell me what to do and how to live my life. They wanted to tell me how to make decisions and what I should and shouldn't be doing.

God thought differently. I do believe I heard Him speak rather clearly to my heart on the matter. I believe that I heard Him ask me a very simple question. It stopped me right in my tracks. I had never been asked anything like it before. "Are you going to listen and do what this person is telling you, or are you going to listen and follow Me?" I believe that was what he asked me straight from the heart. Well, I didn't need to think about it. I knew right then what I was going to choose to do. I knew right then who I was going to choose to follow. I was choosing God. He knew my destination. He knew where He wanted to take me. This human being had no way of taking me there. I would have really missed it and missed the mark by not choosing to go with God.

I had to get out from the chicken coop with the other clucking chickens so that I could fly like the eagle. And that is what I did. I refused to live my life in a cage behind invisible bars, keeping my mouth shut. Eagles soar and fly alone. That was the risk I was willing to take. I made the step that I needed to make for myself and felt very much alone. Oh well! Life goes on. And my dear friend, that was only just the beginning. I was in my thirties and desperate for God. Just the thought of knowing Him brought so much anticipation to my heart—a heart that had been beaten down from the traumas of life, traumas that had been left undone. I was still trying to cover them up. At time I wasn't even conscious of all that was going on. But there was so much happening. And if I would have been told it all right up front my flesh would have most likely said, "No way! I am not signing up for this." I am sure that some go off and sign up for the army without any idea about what they are signing up for. They have signed up to prepare and go off to battle, not knowing at first what to expect. They spend so much time preparing for the battle, defending our country, our nation, our freedom.

Well, there is a real enemy at hand. And one must know how to fight in this spiritual battle. If you don't learn, the enemy will run you over time and time again. People may even lose their lives. The enemy comes to steal, to kill, and to destroy (see John 10:10). Now this particular book is not one that quotes a bunch of Scripture passages. Some people will use their jobs and the titles they carry to feel important. If that is you, then I hope that you do not lose it. Or it could turn out to be the greatest blessing that you have ever gotten. Others may use their bank accounts since they are so stuffed, while others may use a spouse to try to feel significant. A promotion may do it for one, while another may use something entirely different to try to gain fulfillment. People turn to all sorts of things, trying to feel loved, accepted, adored, recognized, etc. Whether you take vacation after vacation or arrange luncheon after luncheon, how have those been working for you? If you lose that thing, what do you do then?

I know all about trying to use one's appearance for acceptance, buying the so-called right type of clothes, shoes, handbags, and other things. If one looks put together on the outside, then perhaps that will fix the inside. Not so. I had it all backward. If you get the inside fixed, healed, and whole, then the outside will shine and function right. What happens when that pretty little face of yours breaks out with a rash? Medication may not work, and it may stay there and haunt you. Then what? If that is your identity and your good looks have been taken from you, who are you without them? That great, long, beautiful hair you once swung around may break and fall out. Then what? If your identity is wrapped up in what you look like, then who are you if you no longer like the way you look? You may have a major problem then. That was me. It was an eye-opener for sure.

In this story, though, Jennifer stood in the department store and had a conversation within herself. And she prayed. She wanted to know her purpose here on earth. What in the world was she supposed to be doing with her life? She was desperate to know. There had to be so much more. She could not run from the idea another day. It would not leave her alone. All the times she tried to run away from the question, it followed her. It was time to get serious. She meant business. Playtime was over. So she prayed her prayer silently before God in real faith. It was a short but straightforward prayer. She wasn't beating around the bush either.

And then she went home. She did not purchase a single thing. Having things is great. It just did not satisfy the longings of her heart.

It seems so very crazy how things can play out at times in one's life. You ask for something, and it seems like you get something that you never asked for, something that you didn't want, something that you didn't sign yourself up for. But boom! It hits you like a tidal wave. And at first, you feel washed out at sea, all alone. But then you realize that you are not alone at all, for He is right there with you.

I found myself in a very undesirable situation. A rash had broken out all over me, and my throat was closing up on me! I was having trouble breathing. I was dizzy, and I began to totally freak out. I was rushed to the emergency room. All of the symptoms stopped, but I could not see the back of my throat. My tongue was so very swollen. It was huge. It looked like a cow tongue. I was still frightened, and I wasn't comfortable going back home after all the treatment that had been given. I should have just camped right out in the ER until the swelling went down. I ended up right back there for a second and a third time. The staff told it was normal for the tongue to remain swollen after people had the reaction to a particular medication. Those doctors could tell me all day long that it was normal, but I felt nothing like normal. I am not so sure that I even had a clue about what normal felt like. Now it is rather funny to think about, but at the time it wasn't so funny.

I wondered, *What in the world is going on and happening to me? I ask God to know Him, to really know Him, and this happens.* Of course, at that particular time, I thought that He was the one who sent me through that lesson, that He was the one responsible for that rash and that allergic reaction. And there is a world full of other people who would believe the same thing I did, namely that God sends diseases and sicknesses to teach us something. I was ignorant. That is the furthest thing from the truth. I had come to the place of knowing that God was not responsible for all of the things that happened in a person's life. And that includes a believing Christian. Not everything that happens to a person is God's will. Now I am not saying that God will not use it. He has used these incidents in my life, but I'm not saying that He caused or allowed them. There is a very big difference. Every decision will lead us somewhere. We all have a choice to make. It is not God's fault when we are not listening to Him. Some refuse to listen, for they do not want to hear or be responsible for what He will say. Others do not listen, for they think they cannot hear Him. Some do not believe He really speaks to one's heart. Some just don't know and will not believe at all.

Not Ready to Go

On March 24, 2008, there she was. Jennifer had been rushed to the ER only to find out she had a serious blood clot in her jugular vein. She received a chest X-ray, and the clot just so happened to show up. That was no coincidence either. No one had been searching for blood clots. She had gone in there with chest pains. Jennifer had been walking around for a few weeks going in and out of medical facilities, complaining about troubling symptoms and leaving without any results. No one knew what the problem was. She knew something was not right. It was so aggravating. Larry was getting annoyed, but not at the doctor's not knowing but rather at me. It was so awful at the time. I wanted to know what it was and how it could be fixed.

As bad as the blood clot appeared, there was a bit of relief. I was not going crazy after all. I knew it. I knew something was not right. And now it had been found out. Finally. It was caught. Immediately, Jennifer was admitted and hooked up to machines—lots of noisy, beeping, monitoring machines. She was told over and over by nurses not to touch her neck where the clot was lodged. It could potentially move upward to the brain or downward right smack into her heart. Either of those movements, and she'd be gone. Just like that. She would be relocated. It was frightening yet confusing to Jennifer. One month prior to this event was the time she had been in the hospital with a full-blown allergic reaction. I had been in very good physical health and was not used to being in and out of hospitals or running off to doctor's offices. This was all very new, and I cannot say that any of it was enjoyable.

I had walked around for years, feeling like something bad and terrible was going to happen to me. It started with a thought. And then the thought kept coming back on a regular basis. It just moved itself right on into my head. I did not ask for its arrival. It just showed up. And I allowed it to stay. I was ignorant and did not realize what was happening to me. That thought made itself rather comfortable and grew stronger in my thinking. Next thing you know, I was trembling in fear, just waiting for it to happen. Like I deserved it. Then in full expectancy of its arrival, I began talking about its arrival to Larry. It did not just pop out from the bushes one night to scare me a little, but it did happen over a course of time.

It had become my confession, and I did get what I had been a confessing. Blood clots are an evil thing. They can and often do kill people. It obviously lost its power over my life. After all, I am still here and writing to you. I am very thankful that my story had a good departure from that hospital room. Shortly after this happened to me, I was told of a woman who went through the same thing and died. She never made it home to her husband and to her children. I cannot even imagine it. Then later on, I was told of another case. The exact same thing happened again, and she did not survive either. I was told over and over that I had been a special case. Many people were praying for me. I even had a godmother—a spiritual one. I was reminded how she would pray and pray for me time and time again. She adored me, and I never understood why. It was just a God thing. Someone once said right in front of me, "I do not see what is so special about Jennifer to make this woman want to be her godmother." I was very young at the time when that was spoken, but I never forgot it. And it wasn't just what was said. It was the how it was said that stung the most.

Attitudes of the heart—now there is a book right there. I have had a share of my own. I made such a big request before a very big God. This situation was not what I had imagined. This again was surely not how God was going to reveal Himself to me, allowing something so terrible to come to me. Well, I did ask for it, not knowing what I was doing. I feared talking about it and expected some bad thing to happen. And it did. Fear or faith—we get to choose. It is up to us, you know. We have a choice and a voice in the matter. We can speak out life, or we can speak out death. Most of us in our ignorant stages have no idea what we are talking about or calling in. This tongue has gotten me into much trouble. If only I had known.

I have prayed big prayers, and I have wanted big answers. I even remember as a child praying and asking God to do something big for me in my life. I wanted Him to do something so big for me so that I would know He was real. I prayed for that in my bedroom when I was a small child. There was no complexity about it. Just a simple prayer prayed in the faith that was inside of me. People can say and think what they choose to think. I had God at a young age. I had Jesus. I believed in Him. I prayed, and my heart believed in Him. I just had no idea about what I had received. That was as far as it went. I had Him, and He was there with me—period. He was there. I just had no idea about who He really was. I knew He was the way to heaven. But who really was this Jesus? And He came with seemingly preposterous benefits. And I wanted to know all about them. I wanted to find out about what was rightfully mine. There was much more to learn.

Later on in life, I received a second filling. I was not even a teenager yet, still just a child. A pastor was praying for me, and while he was praying, something came over me, a warmth that flowed all over. Something was happening, and I did not know what was happening. It was not frightening, even though I did not understand. He did. God did. I did not have to understand it. Faith has nothing to do with understanding. Faith is a heart matter, not a head matter. God knew exactly what I needed. I needed Him and His power. And that is what

I got. I remember that moment very clearly. No question about it. I did not know Him or what He offered or what He was capable of. I did not even know that He was a Him at that time. All I knew was that something happened to me that day, something that would not be taken or stolen from me. That was between me and God. It was my experience with Him. He filled me with the Holy Ghost. He filled me with His power. Then He was there with me for all those years, waiting on me.

Believing in Him was never the issue for me. I believed. That was not my problem. But I kept doubting His love for me. I did not really know and believe that God loved me unconditionally. It was a struggle even after the mercy He had poured out upon me. I was learning of His love through experience. I still had not opened up my Bible. I did not know what He had to say about me. I knew all too well what people had to say. People had their opinions. Some I found out through the grapevine. Others gave me their personal opinions. Some did not have the courage to say anything to my face, so they sent letters. Most of these statements contained so much backstabbing and phoniness. And I no longer do well with being phony. In fact, I hate phonies. I want nothing to do with them. I am past the deceit. I will not settle. I must have the real thing.

I do think it saddened God to watch me struggle in ways. I do believe with all of my heart that it did not amuse Him one bit. I do not think that He thought that it was very funny. I think that it angered Him the way that people laughed at me and made fun of me. I do not believe for one minute that God was jumping up and down, laughing at me too. It was horrifying and humiliating. My doubting and questioning salvation was tormenting. It was going to take a miracle to break me of that tendency. Thinking, wondering, and questioning is not knowing.

The enemy used people. He sent people into my life to try to make me believe that I was not saved, that I was going to hell. It was a nightmare. I was determined to go free, and the war was on. And it was a war—one battle after another. But hey, you cannot have a major victory without a nasty battle to fight through! During those early stages after I began to step out and to trust God, the letters kept coming. It got to the point where I stopped reading them and threw them in the trash right where they belonged! I do believe that God gave me a special dream one night. The dream was so real to me. I woke up patting Larry to see if he was next to me before I could even open up my eyes. I had been raptured in the dream. Jesus did come for me after all. I was saved and I did not get left behind. Those letters were lies sent from the Devil himself. It was just a fear tactic trying to keep me in a state of torment.

Not knowing if God really loves you is tormenting enough. Then not really knowing that you are saved when God says that you are is not living a peaceful life. I could not live in inner peace without getting that straightened out and settled once and for all. My foundation was pitiful. It needed a major makeover. There were too many cracks. It had to be torn apart and restructured. The foundation had to be laid correctly so that it could take on the next level. Building from the foundation up is crucial. The building of my house was a major renovation—a complete do-over.

Like a tree, my roots needed to run deep. When all of the storms hit my life and tried to destroy me, I would not fall over. They could just blow right off from me. I may have bent, but I would not break. I learned fast how to get on my face before God and to pray and to cry out to Him for help. He has always answered. How could He refuse? He always responds to a truthful heart. A real spiritual person is an honest person. You cannot fool God. God is a God of truth. There is no lie in Him.

My life the way I viewed it had not even gotten started. Too much time had been wasted, taken, stolen. I wanted to know about purpose. Why was I born? What was my purpose for being here at this exact time in this present age? Why? And for what? God was the only one who could answer the questions of my heart.

I was not one to sit still. I have known my flesh to be downright lazy, but that does not mean that all it wanted to do was lay around on the couch. I had to constantly be doing something. I kept myself busy. I had my quiet times in the morning, but then off I went. I did not know how to be still. I did not even like stillness. Even with all of the nice homes that Larry and I lived in, I did not really get the chance to just stay at home and enjoy them. I was in and out every day. I did not enjoy my favorite one. After I got it, then it quickly became a burden to me to get it decorated. It was frustrating to me because I struggled with perfectionism. No matter what I did or how I did it, it just never was good enough. It just did not ever look the way I wanted it to look. People would come over and compliment how beautiful it was, and I would still see the imperfections. That is how I viewed my own house, the house that I live in. I saw all that was wrong. I dwelled on all of the wrongness rather than the rightness. My body, this flesh of mine, is my house. It is a temple—a holy temple. The Spirit of the Lord resides in me. This place is only temporary. One day I will be out of here. But I do not want an early departure. Those days for me are over. I desire to live well and to live for God, to stand for Him and to follow Him. I have come to enjoy wearing His royal robe.

When I stand before the Lord, I want to know that I did what I was called to do. I want to leave here satisfied. I want to do what I was born to do for such a time as this. Too much is at stake. I ran for far too long, running from Him and the call. It scared me. I thought that I was just dreaming and imagining something that was not really true. I fought an inward battle. How in the world would God use somebody like me? It baffled my mind. It did not even make sense. I did not know how to do it. I did not even know how to get started in the right direction. But He did.

So I sat there, stuck in that hospital bed with that horrific thing sitting in my neck. Nurses would come in and then leaves. Doctors were coming and going too. Tests here and tests there. Machines were constantly beeping, and there was noise throughout the building.

Hope rode in the front seat of the ambulance. Jennifer remembered how her daughter looked at her and said, "Well, Mommy, this is no time for you to be negative, but the time for you to be positive." Her daughter was just a young child at the time, but she was so very grown up that day. It came out totally unexpected, and Jennifer realized that her daughter listened and paid more attention to her than what she realized. Hope called her daddy to let him know what had happened and what was going on. Larry had rushed out the door that morning, and Jennifer had tried to warn him that something was not right with her. He did not have time to listen. Larry had a business appointment to attend to. He looked at Jennifer as if to say, "Not again! I do not have time to be running off to emergency rooms with you today." So off he went. Now Larry did not actually say those words, but Jennifer knew him well enough to know what he was thinking. She had learned his body language and knew his facial expressions before he could even speak a word. Larry loved Jennifer. I know he did. There's no doubt about it. Not saying that his love was perfect. But it was in a process. It was going to get better and better. He knew how to treat a woman. He was learning how to love his lady. After Larry got the report from our daughter, it did not take him that long to get there.

I know that he felt bad about it. I did not want him to feel bad about it. I cannot say that I even blamed him for not taking that morning more seriously. We had taken so many trips to the ER without any results. But not this one. Finally! Something was going to happen this time. I was not being sent home. I was not expecting to go anywhere anytime soon. Fear tried to grip me. Fear tried to cripple me and shred me to pieces.

My house was not in order. It had only just begun. Too much was out of alignment. My house needed much more than a trip to the chiropractor for an adjustment. Many people need to keep going back to the chiropractor to maintain that alignment. Well, I needed God to align up all that was going on in my life and in my home. Things were out of order. And God is a God of order. And it was going to take more than one trip to my prayer closet. This was not some quick fix either. Not everyone wanted to cooperate. God got a hold of me, and the atmosphere changed. I changed. I was changing for the better. I was undergoing a process, and I know I still am in the process. I now know that I had to be worth something in order for God to put up with me. I do not think that I was an easy one to work with. My heart was willing, but this flesh of mine was a challenge. I am sure that it has been a downright nuisance to some, especially to those who never understood me. I have been very misunderstood. I know that much. But God knows my heart. He sees what all others can't see. And I thank Him for that. I feel that God has swum through many oceans of water to save me, to get through to me, to reach me, to come to me so that I could grab a hold of His hand. Or He grabs a hold of mine. In many things He just had to carry me through. I could not find the steps, so I just relied on Him. He never gave up on me, and I have learned to not give up on Him either.

I did not want another person raising my children. That was one responsibility that I was committed to. I knew that I did not possess the best mothering skills in the world. I did everything I knew how to do and all that I was capable of. I loved to my fullest capacity. The ways I showed love were not always what my children needed. They didn't always need or want me to give them material things. That had been one way I perceived love—giving things. So that is how I tried to love my children for so many years. People, including children, can starve for love all because we do not know how to speak their own individual love language to them. I know with all of my heart that I loved them and still love them. But did they know? I pondered and pondered on that thought, lying there in that bed. Who was going to fight for my children if I wasn't here anymore?

I lived like a little lost sheep, not knowing where my flock was. A major priority in my life was people pleasing, all in the hope of gaining approval. So what happens when those people whose approval you are trying to get don't approve of you? You never feel validated. You never feel approved of, loved, accepted, valued, cared for. You never feel good enough. You do not feel that you measure up.

There has been much that I have wanted to say about and to the victims of sexual abuse to help set them free from turmoil. It's not right. It's not of God. It's not your fault that it happened to you. You are not to blame. You did not ask for it, and you didn't deserve it. You do have legal rights. You do have spiritual rights as well. Just because one is called to forgive, that does not mean for one minute that you do not need to report it, to expose it and to stop it from happening to another person. Again, I say that God did not call me out to carpet sweep. I was stuck in that far too long. God came and picked up the carpet and dragged out all the trash so that I could clean up my mess. You can only pile so much under the rug until it starts showing. The rug on the inside of me could not handle any more carpet sweeping. I was responsible for my own life, not another human being. I needed to break free so that I could make choices of my own, choices that I wanted to make. I had been choosing to ignore what my heart was telling me for too long. It was my life to live. It was not another's. Other people will not answer to God for me or you. I will answer for me, and you will answer for you. We are not playing the blame game before God. And there is a time to grow up and take responsibility for one's own actions and choices. Time is not something you can get back, and I do not want to waste it. It is a gift.

I've learned how victims of sexual abuse are taught that their needs are not important. They feel that what's done to you does not matter because they are not important and they do not matter. They may not even acknowledge that they have needs at all. They are just there to exist and to please others.

Pretending that it never happened does not fix the pain. It will not heal you. And it will take a lot of pretending in many different areas. You get lost somewhere in the midst of all of that pretending. You lose yourself. You are not being true to yourself by pretending. Even if you do not know who the real you is. It is better to find out than to spend an entire life trying to be something you are not. Be true to yourself. It is time you set yourself free. We are not responsible for another's actions. But we are responsible for our own. We can be like the prophet who proclaimed peace and yell from the rooftops, "Peace, peace," but there is no peace. You won't have peace living a lie. It just will not happen for you. God is not a liar. God is a God of truth.

Each do-over has shown me that this was not ready to be released. It would had been a complete embarrassment. I was not ready. I was still in a process. I needed to start again. One copy was so very long that Larry had commented that I had written an entire bible. My version. It was for me. All of this writing it out, talking it out, thinking it out has really gotten it out. Gotten it out of me. I do not even want to discuss it anymore. I feel so over talking about it. It has become old news to me. It is not something that I want to keep reliving. I am ready to drop it. I thought that many times only to find myself rehashing the same things over and over again. I needed to talk about it. If I had to cuss it all out, then that's what I needed to do. I just had to get it out. It had to come out. I needed to grieve all that had taken place, and I did. It was the only way to get past it. God did not instantly just zap me out from it. He had me work through it with Him.

I have overcome! Glory hallelujah! I am free. I have gotten past it. I no longer feel the need to lash out the way I have lashed out on paper or through typing. The times I was not heard in the matter did make it harder for me. I was overlooked and ignored. It was so disgusting to me, and the whole idea of not being heard or believed made it so much harder for me to truly forgive. I was threatened not to tell people, but I told them anyway, many of which did not believed. How bad that felt cannot even be put into words.

You cannot truthfully forgive someone in your own heart when you cannot even remember what they did to you. That is another reason it has to be exposed and dealt with. It will sit there, festering inside of you. You may leave and get out from the traumatizing wrong that someone did to you. You may escape from a life that you were not called to live. You may get out and away from unhealthy people. You may be entirely removed from the situation. You may have thought that it is all forgotten, and you may have pretended it never took place. But the real truth is that it did. It did happen, and it needs to come out into the open where it is once and for all *exposed*. Then truth prevails. Then healing and dealing comes. Grieving time is very healthy and necessary, especially if you ever hope to be truly free. One's dream may be another's nightmare. God will be with you. He is the only healer who can heal a wound like that.

Forgiveness is a choice. It is not based off of a feeling. I cannot think of one time that my flesh felt like forgiving someone for a wrong done to me. I choose to forgive because God has forgiven me time and time again. He asks me to forgive those who have abused me and done me wrong so that I no longer have to suffer. Forgiving sets one free. Depending on the offense, the offender, and what that person meant to you, sometime forgiving may take longer than other times. It starts with a choice. Then you must allow God to heal the broken, wounded heart. He will lead you. We need His guidance, and we need His counsel. There is no other love that melts the heart like His. He knows what we need and right when we need it. He may choose to use others to love you and get you through it all. But He should be your primary source, the one to whom you run.

God knew all of those times when I thought, *Well, this one is it*. He knew better. He was protecting me. We can be so foolish at times. I will speak for myself. I have been so very foolish because

I didn't want to wait. And most every time I took off like a wild horse running, I got myself into trouble—trouble that I did not want—all because I was impatient. This patience thing has been one of the most difficult processes, but I have chosen to *cooperate*. Rather than keep ignoring undesirable circumstances, I have learned and continue to learn that patience pays off in the long run. Wanting something right now is not to be trusted. Patience has been working inside of me and changing things in me that I never even knew existed. It can be rather amazing what all can come up from the heart when one is *waiting*.

I began to see something in me that perhaps I could have very easily overlooked if I had not been called to wait. "THE LONGER THE LEFT THE HIGHER THE RIGHT." I got that from a previous pastor who helped me grow by leaps and bounds in knowing the real, true nature of Christ. I was led right to his campus. No doubt about it. I was in right place at exactly the right time. I was desperate. I have visited many desperate places in my lifetime. If you reflected over my life, you would think that I was already a hundred-year-old lady with gray hair. Not that I feel old. I am not old. Nor do feel old. I just feel that I have lived through some major obstacles I've had to overcome. It has been one obstacle course right after another. The beauty of it is that now I know the truth. I know the real God. I praise Him for who He really is. And I can praise Him even when my heart is hurting because I know He loves me. I know that He cares. I have discovered what the sacrifice of praise is all about. When you just do not feel like you have one ounce of praise left inside of you, you can decide to turn to Him anyhow, and something miraculous comes up. You begin to praise—whether in a song or just a whisper. It begins to change your heart. Peace begins to come over you and around you. You then find yourself in a completely different atmosphere, a more desirable one. You lose sight of all that was troubling you. And you're caught up in a glory that is simply amazing.

You cannot put it into words. It's just simply amazing. It is glorious. His glory is there. Hallelujah!

Praise has helped me overcome being an angry white woman. After the pretending stopped, after I was free to stop it, I got angry! *Very, very, very angry.* I was finally allowed to feel. It was now okay to really feel what I was feeling without being forced to feel that I was wrong for feeling the way I felt. You may even have hatred toward someone. But you may have never been allowed to say it or to feel it or express it because it was so very wrong. Christians don't do that, right? They're not supposed to hate anyone except the Devil. You cannot deal with your emotions or be honest with God or yourself if you are not given permission to really feel. I did not want to feel wrong. I know all too well what it was like trying to say the right words or do the so-called right things all in the hope of not being wrong. I was not honest with myself because I did not want to be wrong.

What happens, though, when you find out that you were the one who was right? And it was so very freeing to finally allow myself to feel. I was able to be honest with myself and what I was really feeling inside. I had deeper pains than I had ever realized, and I had some hatred. I was pretending that I had forgiven when there was no way that was really true.

I had so many do-overs in writing this book. Each time more and more release came forth. It was as if I was getting freer and freer each time around. There was a hidden life that I was not permitted to talk about it. It had been stuffed so far down inside of me. It was buried. It was time to get all of it completely out. Then I would be totally free from it. I would no longer feel that I needed to keep on talking about it. There was far too much at stake. There was much more to my life. I was letting go of the past by finally talking about it, grieving, and healing. Then I went through a process of choosing to accept reality. Child molestation is evil. And the effects on me were downright traumatizing. No wonder I made some of those bad choices throughout my life. The reasons behind some of the horrific events that had taken place in my life now became so obvious to me—how I felt about myself, how I saw myself. It explained all of the pain from self-doubting, never measuring up. It became so very crystal clear to me. All of the confusion was brought out into the light. It was exposed. It no longer had power over me. The insecurities finally made sense. Then there was the shame about who I thought I was. Some say that the victims of sexual abuse never totally free themselves from the damages. Without God's help, I do not see how it could ever happen. Pills cannot heal a wound like that.

So then I needed to choose to let go of all that could have been. And that was very hard for me. It was a very difficult process. I had even felt stuck there. Much forgiving was needed. I needed to forgive myself too. That was the most difficult part of all. But I had to get past this before the next chapter of my life could begin. If I had not chosen to cooperate, I'd still be a prisoner in my own body. I'd be living in bondage, tormented day after day, night after night, wishing nothing would change. God was so good to me through it all. If it had not been for His goodness than I wouldn't have made it. I'd been stuck, never breaking free and becoming what I dreamed I could be.

I had many health problems during this process. These undesirable symptoms that did not want to leave me alone. I had much to deal with. I once felt that I needed a man, but then I no longer wanted one. A medical doctor told me that the reason I had all of the symptoms in my body was due to my unhappiness. He sure did tell me that. It was true. I went through a short time of being very dissatisfied and very unhappy. I was grieving over my loss. I was a very angry white woman. I had bitterness in my heart. And I was mad!

I did have a Christian therapist during that time frame. It was not anything to be laughing about either. God sent me there for a divine purpose. God used that person to help me. I was in a very critical condition. I needed the counsel, the safe place, and the support to get through it all. Someone who has not had this experience will never understand what a person goes through when this sort of evil happens. God did not just zap me out from my pain like I had wanted. I had the faith that a miracle would occur. That was not the issue. The issue was me. I did not want to hurt anymore. I did not want to feel pain anymore. I wanted to be zapped and fixed by God.

Much prophecy had been communicated to me about the plans that God had for my life, and not just in certain meetings. It came from many different places as well as from God Himself. He spoke to me. And that was what mattered the most. He was there beside me during it all. He was speaking to me and telling me what to do. I just did not understand Him. But I learned.

I have come to learn all about this flesh of mine. And now understand the major difference between my flesh and my spirit. That is a war at hand all by itself. Oh, yes, they war with each other. My flesh is so weak and not very cooperative. And my spirit is the willing one. The spirit in me is more than willing to serve God and do what He asks of me. This flesh part wants to be lazy and passive. I do not mean that it was to lie around on the sofa and eat popcorn either. This flesh can be downright stubborn, especially when there is no emotional support for what I have been instructed to do. It is easier to give into this flesh and make excuses, not following and doing what you know you should do. Reasoning and doubting are not faith. I have been called to live a life of faith. God responds to faith, not reason.

The many times I was instructed to write this book again, my flesh rose up and said, "No way! Not again." It did not want to choose to listen at first and go through it all over again. Surely, that cannot be God. I would have preferred to throw the laptop right out the window. I did not want to cooperate. My spirit in me was willing. That is what I chose to go with. The spirit part inside of me knew better. It knew how to follow. I have been tested and tested and then tested some more.

There have been some major tests in my life. I have the ability inside of me to pass all of the tests that keep coming, and so do you.

I know what it means to say, "Oh, God, I will follow You anywhere and do whatever You want me to do." Then you may find yourself being asked to do something that you do not want to do. Nothing in you wants to cooperate except for the spirit part of you. We live in bodies. Like a car, it takes you where you need to go. This body is the shell one lives in. Some are larger than others. Everyone has a different type. But we all have a spirit, a soul, and a body. The soul in a person is the mind, the will, and the emotions. It is where the "I do not want to. I do not feel like it" comes from. That is where all the reasoning comes from. You listen to that, and it will be an absolute miracle to ever get up and do what God says. Many are called, but few are chosen, for few will choose to follow.

My life has not been an easy one. I have not always been able to go out and buy everything all up either. I know about shopping in secondhand stores and wearing used shoes. I once put something on the layaway plan. I know how to dig for what I am searching for. I know how to treasure hunt. I have enjoyed myself in those environments on many occasions. My heart was thankful, not grumbling and complaining, not looking for entitlement for all that I had been doing for such a great cause.

I have had my highs and my lows. And then some lowers. This flesh can be downright stubborn. It can get one into a world of trouble. It will constantly talk about how it feels and will speak despair and defeat when the spirit inside of me is all about the victory. I know all about it.

On the other hand, I have had a world of high-end things, none of it satisfying me. It just did not have the power to fill me. There was no power in it to help me. None of the stuff caused me to rise up and to dance, to shout, or to sing. They didn't give me a heart that was bursting forth with real and lasting joy. It did not work for me. It just left me in need. *Stuff* can be just great, but it is not the place, the source where I draw my life from. If it were, then I'd be dead.

If I, Jennifer, would have waited for all of my so-called conditions to have been just right just the way that I had wanted, then I most likely would still be waiting to get started, not doing what I needed to be doing.

I have come to the place of really believing that my God does have my best interest at heart. He does so much to protect me. It is up to me to follow His lead. It is my choice to choose whether or not I will listen and not to run out ahead of Him. What a hurtful mess that has brought. It is my job to pay enough attention to Him, to wait on Him and not to move until He says move. And when He does say to move, I must make sure I go in the direction He says. With specific instructions, He gives out the when, the how, but not always the why. If He always told us why, then we would not need much faith.

In the finer houses that Larry and I had purchased, there was a cleaning crew to come into the homes for cleaning. They were too large for one person to get the job done right in one day. And I had my share with cleaning. I was scrubbing showers and the water closets! Cinderella's prince had come, so those days were over for me. Hallelujah! But I believe there came a time when God had to deal with me concerning my children. They were spoiled. They received too many things, and they didn't have many chores. There was nothing for them to clean because the cleaning crew always picked up after them. They were supposed to keep their rooms straightened up. I had stopped doing so. They were perfectly capable of making up their beds and picking their clothes up off of the floor and putting them away. They did learn how to do their own laundry. I was not their maid but their mother. When it came to the tidiness of their own personal space, those two could prove a challenge.

I just could not seem to get past this particular issue that I believed God was telling me. It was just taking me quite some time to really get it and to act on it. My little princess Hope said to me, "Mom, there is no way that I will ever scrub a toilet! That is gross. I do not clean toilets." Well, the time did come for her to use a scrub brush on one. She did clean it after all. It was a very large wake-up call for that little precious daughter of mine.

Mysterious Woman
Meets Wise Guy

That was how Larry and I began. That was how he saw me and that was how I viewed him. I was not even looking. It just happened. I walked into the room, and suddenly, there was a moment. He came walking toward me. I did not just fall into his arms and live happily ever after either. Now that would be a fantasy. He was different from any other man I had met in person before. It did not take very long for me to realize. This entire chapter of my life was similar to some of those movies I had once been so fascinated with.

It was not even something that I could have dreamed. I did have a wild imagination, but not even this had crossed my mind before. People thought that I had gone mad. I was only twenty-four years old. I wanted to break free from the place I had felt stuck in. It was nothing but a bad memory to me. I was so over it. I did not consider myself a runner. Running was never my thing. It hurt my knees. I would have gladly been gracious in working through issues. I would have preferred being honest and truthful. I did not do well with being phony.

An opportunity came for me, and I took it. It thrilled me to no end. I packed up and left. I moved out. Just like that. I cannot think of one person who supported me in this. I was on my own. But that was what my heart bled for. I know that my papa was in shock. He was even more shocked that I did not ask him for any money. This new man in my life took care of the bill. He paid for the moving trucks, and he was taking care of me. I felt at that time that I had just found my ticket to heaven. Now this would mean that I no longer had to run to Papa and hear the same sentences that he spoke to me over and over again. He would give me money to pay for the things that I needed and wanted. But it was not a free gift to me. It came with a condition. He wanted me to keep silent and not rock the boat in the mad waters that kept me stirred up all the time. Papa wanted peace all around him with everyone. He kept a phony peace, which I could not stand. And he was famous for making excuses for people, including me. He was a Christian man. He was brought up in the hills of Alabama. He was a country boy, and he wasn't ashamed of it either. That is where I get some of that sweet home Alabama from. I have some of that Southern flare in me. I enjoy watching those ladies from the South and the way they would strut around in those very large hoop dresses. They knew they were something, and they were.

Papa did not remain there in Alabama. He packed up and left. He followed what He believed was God, and he and my grandmother moved away. He got away from his kindred folk. I do not know if that was what he was trying to do, but he did move off to another state without any of them. It was there that he became blessed with his own business. The only advertising came through the word of mouth. He would tell me that he was a very blessed man. I believed him. He was my hero.

In my eyes he was not perfect, and his ways of doing things weren't perfect either. But one thing was for certain. I knew that he loved me. Even to this day, I believed that I was his favorite. We just had a special relationship even in the midst of all of the dysfunction. I knew that I could count on him when I needed him. I knew that he would show up when he said he would be there. Papa would not abandon me. He fought for me like I was his very own child. I believe that he loved me to his very core. I looked to him as my own father regardless of what any other person thought about it or how anyone tried to make me feel about it.

Back in those days, I did not understand a thing about spiritual battles. I did not know that the Devil was a spiritual outlaw or that he was behind all of the evil that people had done to me. I didn't know that he was the one behind the scenes who was using certain people, trying to keep me silent and prevent me from ever finding my own voice. My enemy did not want me talking. It was better for him if I would just sit there and look pretty, not saying a word. It was a very shallow life. There was so much more buried inside to discover about myself. Walls would need to come down. Those invisible walls that one can build up to keep those hurtful people out keep the person locked inside too. It was time to break free. I felt like a prisoner. I was beginning to realize that I did not have to remain one. Meeting Larry was the beginning of the healing process. I do believe that God was using him, and he did not even know it. He was a heathen man at that time. He did not stay that way very long though when I waltzed into his world. So it was going both ways. God used me to get through to Larry. And God was using Larry to provide for me with natural provisions, lifting me up high on some sort of pedestal. The red carpet was rolled out for me. And I must say that I liked it very much! I felt important and special. I felt valuable.

When I walked into the room, Larry took notice. And others could not help but take notice because Larry was not quiet about it. Papa used to be that way too. He would make a big fuss over me. "Here comes my good-looking granddaughter." That was my papa. I really did enjoy all of the attention that I received from him. And I did enjoy the attention that Larry gave to me as well. It made me feel that I mattered. God's grace was most definitely upon us. The way that we came together was not ideal. The circumstances around our meetings were not very desirable whatsoever. But we do have a story. God does forgive—that's for sure. God does heal for certain. And God does make up for wrongs that have been done to a person. He did bless us regardless of what anyone else had to say. He sure did. Glory to my God!

I certainly did not know beforehand what I would be called to endure. I did not know what I had signed up for, and neither did Larry. I was willing to overlook certain things in the beginning. But as time progressed, those things turned into monstrous things that irritated me and annoyed me and rubbed against me like a piece of sandpaper. Time ran its course, and I was at a place where I could not take it anymore and I wanted change. Our entire relationship has been a learning lesson—a time to grow and to mature, a time of patience and much forgiveness. And it certainly gave me an opportunity to exercise my faith. My faith muscles did get extensive workouts. The results that I desired and prayed for came. They did not come overnight either. Time was involved. There was much waiting. That was not something that my flesh liked. It did not want to be bothered with waiting. "Just give it to me now." That was more like it. And I did learn, and I am still learning about this thing called patience. Faith and patience go hand in hand. I know all about it now. I have had my own little fits along my way. I still knew how to act like a child with God. There were many times when I looked like a little girl with pigtails, whining to get her way. I have come far enough with Him that I am comfortable being real with Him. I can be totally honest with Him, even if I am wrong. Then He can make it right. The price has already been paid.

I went from a little mouse voice to a lion's roar. And boldness did come out from me. I went from trophy wife to warrior!

I feel as if I have learned every dance there is to dance with this man of mine. I've learned to move to the music that has played on in my life. I am fascinated with the tango, even though I have not physically danced that one out. I would not mind learning that one though!

You cannot fight spirits and the Devil with a loaded gun! I did not understand just how evil and cunning that Devil was. There is no truth in him whatsoever. He knows Scripture better than a lot of people too. He sure did mess with my mind. He twists and distorts the real truth into something evil. He tries to trick people and lead them astray right into his traps. He sets up ambushes all around. Many do not see them until it is too late. I was called out to confront certain situations with certain individuals. That was God. But since I had struggled with double-mindedness, the enemy had a field day with me. I was only beginning to learn what God was and wasn't. There are many voices in this world. Many need to be told to shut up. Shortly after the confronting I was back apologizing for it. Oh, yes, the Devil was behind that and had me go and apologize and take responsibility for another's actions—all for the sake of love. I had much to learn on this subject called love.

I had a heart that was desperate to please. I wanted to please God at any cost. If I could just manage to do everything right and do exactly what He required of me then I would be right. That kept me on a constant merry-go-round. It was exhausting too. And I did find out that God was not the one behind it either. I was already right with Him. I had Jesus, and Jesus had me. And that made me right. It was all about receiving. It had nothing to do with me being on a work cycle. Religion was still at play.

I began to see that Devil for what he was really about and how he operated. He is a liar. That is for sure. Never in my life did I think that he could do what he did to me. Even as a Christian, I had not been taught about him. I got to learn about him the hard way—all by experience.

In the very early beginning stages of my relationship with Larry, I was used to seeing him in slacks, a dress shirt, and guinea shoes. But one day we met for lunch. I miraculously arrived earlier than him. I was waiting inside of my BMW. Larry pulled in and got out from his vehicle. He was wearing jeans and a white T-shirt. His dress shirt was hung up in the back. That was when I really saw him. He had warrior arms. He had the frame of a well-put-together man. I saw him as a real man that day. I felt safe with him. He knew how to use a pistol. Let's leave it at that.

I got to go and live in a place that I had only dreamed of before. It was inside of a gated apartment community. A brand-new one, I will add. I liked new. This wouldn't be a big deal for some, but for me at that particular time in my life, it was a dream come true. It was in a location that I was fascinated with. And now I was there. People thought that I had lost my mind. Some even tried to tell me that I was crazy. One person said that I had done what she could only think about doing but was too afraid to ever pursue. What is the point of having any dreams if you never get to experience them?

I was going to enjoy the journey to the fullest for as long as it lasted. And I did. Regardless of the pain, regardless of the jealousy that was around me, regardless of all the naysaying, I was going for it. It was a chance at life—my life. Someone actually wanted me, and some people had a very hard time accepting that. True colors began to show. And it was not pretty, not to me. I am still on the journey too. It has kept on going.

Larry did come to my rescue. He did sweep me off from my feet. He put a genuine smile on my face. He brought me fresh excitement. My foot really did fit the shoe! I have my own story with the glass slipper. Larry would always tell me—and he still tells me to this day—that I was the one he always hoped for. I was the person he could only dream about meeting. It is really nice to be wanted. It is really nice to be cared for. It is really nice to be cherished. It is very nice to be loved. To know that you are loved is a lovely and remarkable thing to me. I am loved. I got to experience real, genuine love.

The first day in the courtroom, an army was there for battle. Everyone was staring right at me, trying to cause me to turn back in fear. I had no idea that I had been set up to endure my very own David and Goliath story. I was fighting for my only child at that time. I did not know how to put on the armor of God. I did not know how to dress for this battle. I did not have any preparation time to prepare for this. It happened so very quickly, and I was just in it. As much as I hated the idea of a long, drawn-out custody battle, it was fight or die. That is how I saw it. I had no choice but to fight. The opposing side was not going to let me walk away, not the way that I wanted.

I chose to stand up on the inside and face my fear and my enemies head-on and fight for what was right. And I did. It felt uncomfortable. It was not something that I wanted to do. I was at the place in my life when I no longer wanted anything to do with those people who rose up against me. I was ready to let it be my past. I wanted to move onward and forward, leaving all of those undesirable details behind me. What had appeared to be so pretty and attractive in the very beginning turned into complete ugliness. The guy even looked at me in the mirror, compared himself to me, and told me that he was prettier than me. It was quite awful. I did not want to exercise any sort of patience during this battle. I wanted to walk and be done with it just like that. I didn't want to go through what I had to go through in order to get the results I wanted. You cannot be a giant killer without a giant to kill! What more can I say?

Wax On, Wax Off

I lived with my grandparents for some of those teenage years. One day I got a wild idea in my head to go out and wax my car. It was a hot summer day. Getting the wax on and making a big mess was no problem for me. I do not recall reading the instructions. That was not my way of doing things. I was not a reader in those days anyway. I just did it. Then I walked away and left my car sitting out in the sunshine, baking with wax all over the hood. When I returned, I noticed that the wax was stuck. I could not get it off. I was unable to clean up the mess that I had made all over my car. I needed a stronger arm. I had to get someone else to clean it up and make it new again. Papa came to my rescue. I could wax on in more ways than putting wax on a car too. Then Papa would come to the rescue and wax it all off—mess cleaned up, mess wiped away, mess all gone. There were times I did need to be rescued. Not everything that Papa did for me enabled me.

My Cinderella story with Larry all began in a place I had once dreamed of—Palm Beach, Florida. There was just something about those palm trees that fascinated me. They appeared to be prettier there. Perhaps the branches looked greener. The sky and the ocean looked different through my eyes. I even liked the sand better there when it was stuck between my toes. The air felt fresher. I enjoyed the breeze. Back then the wind couldn't blow through my hair since it was covered with hair spray. It would not move. It was stuck in the same style, stiff as a board. That was how I felt—stiff. I did not know how to relax. What was that? I had no clue.

The mall was just simply grand to me. And the church that I found myself sitting in was like being in church for the very first time. It was far more than just sitting there and taking up space in a chair. At the church I met a beautiful older woman I came to adore. She had met with me once, and I began to spill out some of the pain that was tormenting me. She immediately recognized it. It was very familiar to her. She knew what it was and where it came from. Tears streamed down my cheeks. She did get to see me cry, but I did not mind, not with her. She spoke out to me with a soft voice. She was a lady who came across with such a gentle and loving spirit. She then told me something that I had not ever heard before, something I've never forgotten. "God does not condemn you. *He meets us right where we are.*" It was if she was speaking a foreign language to me. But it sounded so glorious. It was inviting and caused me to want to come closer. I no longer felt the need to run away from God. He was using this woman to draw me closer to Him. Up to that point, I had not known anyone like her. It was a very new and fresh beginning for me.

She became a prayer warrior for me and prayed me through that David and Goliath story. I know she had many others praying for me as well. Prayer changes things. Prayer works. God does hear the cries of a humbled heart. He does answer.

I honestly did not know back then what God would do for me. I hoped. I wanted to believe for good and not for evil. I had no written word to stand on. It was faith I had on the inside of me. Perhaps it was the size of a mustard seed. I kept looking back at myself and all that I had done. People did not want to allow me the chance to forget it either. Certain ones enjoyed being constant reminders to me. I just wanted to shut them off and enjoy some silence. God knew my heart, and that was all that mattered. I had much rejection to work through. I had extensive people-pleasing skills. I did not need a book to teach me that. This whole idea on what a love walk looked like had to be torn apart and done completely over. What I had thought before was entirely wrong. I had been duped and deceived. What I had been taught that God expected or desired for me was false. In fact, He led me in the opposite direction through a much smaller and narrower gate.

I got to learn about boundaries for the very first time. I had a new picture going on inside of my head—a pretty house with a white picket fence all around it and beautiful fresh flowers all around with such a fragrant scent. This house did not have stink in it. And my fence had a gate with a lock on it. My front door was no longer left wide open for all of the intruders and undesirables to come prancing right in. I arose with a boldness and slammed the door shut on that misery.

I am enjoying me. I no longer hate myself but now can honestly say that I do love being me. I would not want to be another. I would not want another's life. I appreciate my own. I am thankful for my own. That is a miracle. I can truthfully say that I love myself. I love Jennifer. God taught me how to love myself in a healthy way by believing everything He had to say to me. I do not need anyone else's ministry. Nor would I want or covet another's now. I have been given my very own. And I have no desire to be someone's clone.

Not all people were interested in my dreams. I did eventually learn that it was better not to tell others about my dream. It had never crossed my mind that some things were between me and God. I did have precious pearls given to me directly from Him. Some people didn't appreciate all He had shared with me. Some of the people I thought would be happy for me were not very happy about it at all. There are some people out there who are glad for you as long as you are not doing better than them. As long as you do not pass them up, so be it. And there are some who do not want you doing well at all. They feel superior to you as long as you stay down. And I did eventually find those who would rejoice with you. Who will believe with you? Who will praise with you? Who shares a like-minded faith? Iron sharpens iron. I prefer to surround myself with those I consider real family.

I did get to experience firsthand casting my precious pearls out there before the swine! It was like giving a Mercedes to pigs—pigs getting their filth all over a luxury item, not knowing how to treat it. A pig does not know the value of a Mercedes. I do see myself as luxurious, for I believe that I am of God. And God has given me my very own dream. It comes straight from heaven right into my heart. I have been through difficult seasons where my flesh wanted to say, "I did not sign up for this. This was not what I had asked for or what I had expected." My flesh has wanted to bolt. This has been an ongoing process. It has brought many tears. I've had to face my fears one battle after another, fighting some alone with only God. I did learn that you are never really alone. He is there. And He is all one needs. When I needed another person, God would send one. God did become my source. Not all the people were intended to stay. God used them for His purpose, and the journey continued on. The Devil sent some people too. I learned the difference between good and bad people. I made up my mind a long time ago that if it came down to me having to stand alone with God, then that was exactly what I was determined to do. If none wanted to choose to go with me, then I would still choose to follow Him.

I have genuine laughter in my heart and home now. Laughter has become part of my daily life. I was able to lighten up and to enjoy the life given to me. Larry had been the ball of laughter, and I had been the very serious one. We did learn how to work through our differences together. It has taken time and continual work and commitment, but now we get to enjoy the fruit of our labor. There was no way that I was going to have a phony marriage where I couldn't be real or communicate. That was something that I was not willing to sacrifice. It was a great need. I am thankful that the Lord helped me endure to the day when I did begin to see the change happen. I am glad that I did not give up and stop believing. I am thankful that God changed and healed my heart and also appreciate the man I managed to keep. With God's help of course. The whole thing on feeling that I had to have one, meaning a man then going to not wanting one at all. That was a season all by itself—a long one that was not so very enjoyable. God has been working inside of me. That is for sure. I am so very thankful for a certain friend God gave to me who was also a mother. She is so very special to me. Our paths crossed in Georgia, and just at the right time too. She let me vent all the many times that I needed a good venting. Most women I know are like that. We need to just let it all out at times. I know all about standing true to my confession ... and standing in the faith. I am a faith lady. I believe, and I have faith. I just know that there were times when I needed to let loose without anyone making me feel bad or judging me. We still have this flesh thing about us, and mine has pitched some tantrums! I could get so mad at this man of mine. I mean, really mad. But then miraculously, God would deal with me. He would help me. He would listen to me. He would show up for me. And then somehow I could not wait to make up with him. It's crazy but true.

I have learned to relax and to allow God to take the load off. I was never meant to carry those loads anyway. They were far too heavy. It allows me to stay in peace and remain in a happy state. Being anxious and fretting always led me in the wrong direction, which would bring some undesirable symptoms. Now I recognize when I am getting overly frustrated and imbalanced. I will fight for my place of peace. I have no desire to live in misery and discontent. I also came to a place in my life years ago where I enjoyed silence. I enjoyed being quiet and sitting quietly before the Lord. I wanted to hear Him. I desired Him and His manifested presence. I wanted Him to reveal Himself to me. And He did. He has since then too. And there is nothing else like Him.

Many of the things and attacks that once moved me no longer affect me. They seem so very petty. They're not even worth talking about. I have gone through one fire after another. I have been taught how to fight, not in my own strength and not with physical weapons.

You cannot fight the Devil with a pistol! You must fight spirits with the Holy Spirit. I win. The Lord is my Helper. He causes me to rise up and stand in His power. I can rely on His power in times when I need to keep quiet! *Selah!* Pause and think of that. He has taught me what it means to rest and trust in Him. My mouth has gotten me into too much trouble. I have learned from this mouth of mine. I know of certain times when I was speaking death and other times when I chose to speak life. There is an entire book right there on that particular subject—my very own mouth.

It amazes me that we can choose what we are calling in ourselves just by choosing to talk right. Not only did I learn this for myself, but I do believe that God taught me this principle about prophesying over my children. When they went through their own dark hours and acted all crazy, I was instructed to stop speaking out about what my son was doing and begin to speak about what I wanted to see and what God had to say about him. Eventually, after some time passed, the entire situation turned around. It worked. God's word will always return power. It was spoken out with a heart of faith. I obeyed the instruction given to me. I was so happy with the outcome. I was so very thankful. What if I had chosen not to have listened to what God was speaking to me? Then who would be to blame for the outcome? The situation could have ended up with a death. I chose life. I spoke life. I yelled out life. I cried life with tears. Life, life, life was in me. I had faith for life! I did see life. Praise the Lord!

It has become obvious to me that there will be those who say they cannot hear God or do not think that God speaks to them. Not all but some just do not want the responsibility of hearing Him. They fear what may be required. They choose to not hear Him. So whose fault is that? God is a gentleman, and He will not force His will or Himself on any human being. That is just not going to happen. That is not His nature.

Then I have had another experience with types of people who claim they hear God and follow Him. I am not about to play their judge either. I know we've been warned and need to be aware of types who are roaming around out there. A person can say all sorts of things. What does the fruit show to you? God does and will give us discernment to recognize what we need to know and protect us. We do not have to know the why behind the instruction when we trust the one who is giving it. We may learn the reason later and be so glad that we listened in the first place. I can now look back at those undesirable years and see so many times when I believed God was speaking to me. But I did not know His voice. It was not a loud voice. It was gentle, and it came from within me. He would speak to my heart. He was there! He had been there all along.

The Healer in Me

On March 26, 2008, at around four o'clock in the morning, I was awakened. It was not easy getting into a deep sleep in that hospital room. There was too much noise all around me. I felt a prompting to sit up.

This happened shortly after I had prayed my big prayer in faith a month after the ER event with the allergic reaction. A month later we found the blood clot. My grandfather had dealt with blood clots in his body. He had to take medications for them. Once, he had a very close call and almost died. I do remember secretly praying for him to live and not die. I could not have imagined my life back then without my hero. He was the hero of my story. What more can I say?

At this time in the hospital, I still hadn't begun to read my Bible and gather all the information inside its pages. But I had begun a new journey and taken up reading. I was on my second book from a well-known author, a Christian woman who was also a minister. I had an instant connection with her. I felt it. I could relate. And she encouraged me. If it hadn't been for this woman, I cannot imagine how my life would have gone. God used her to fan the flames within me. Some of her personality traits reminded me of myself. So there were parts that were funny to me. I could see myself going through certain events that she spoke of. It felt safe, even though she was not actually present.

Watching her on television had become a part of my life. I learned from her. She was genuine and real. That is also what drew me in. I hated phonies, and I was no longer interested in sitting under some rigid law-abiding system.

So at four o'clock in the morning, I followed the prompting that I felt and opened up this woman's book to the place where I had left off at home. Right at the very top of the page was just what I needed at the right time. There was a Scripture passage waiting for me to see it. It was taken from Philippians 4:6 (AB). "Do not fret or have any anxiety about anything, but in every circumstance and in everything, by prayer and petition (definite requests), with thanksgiving, continue to make your wants known to God."

I had not ever seen a verse like that before. It began to thrill my heart. I pondered on it. Then I found myself praying. The verse told me not to fret or have anxiety about anything. Back then I was a very anxious human being. It had become such a part of my life I did not even recognize it. I did not know of any other way to live at that time. I was ignorant in many ways but willing to learn. I did have a teachable spirit. I was very thankful and told God so. The doctors had located the clot, but it hadn't been something they had been looking for either. It just so happened to show up in the chest X-ray. To me that was a miracle right there. The woman who did the X-ray for some reason did not have it aligned accurately, and it had taken the shot of the blood clot. Now that was God. I do believe somehow He was very much involved behind the scenes. That was no coincidence to me. God's angels could have very easily shifted that screen and put in the right position so that we could find the clot. I do not know how He did it, but I believe He did.

One of the physicians told me that his friend dropped dead in the front yard from a blood clot. Then there was this woman technician who was running a test on me as she talked about her father's experience with blood clots. She went on to tell me that I did not need to have anything to do with them! I did not want its existence! People kept saying I was a special case. I was informed that people didn't often get blood clots in their jugular veins without some sort of head injury or head trauma. What had happened to me was very unusual. They had not seen anything like this before.

All sorts of thoughts ran through my head. I did not have any head trauma. I was thinking bad thoughts, but I had no type of head injury. It was a mystery to them.

I had never prayed the way I did that time at four in the morning. It felt so awesome. This boldness came out of me. I mean, real boldness. I was doing what the Scripture said for me to do. I was thankful, not fretting over it at the time, and I was very definite and specific with my request. I even began to speak out confidently how I was His child and how I did not have to put up with that mess. I did not want to have to live by some sort of strenuous diet plan and be on medications. I didn't want someone to stick a very long needle in my abdomen and give me an injection every day. And I certainly did not want to wait six whole months to see if that thing would dissolve. I mean, really. I wanted to go home, healed. Period. No doubt about it. That was what I wanted, and that was the exact thing that I asked for.

These doctors start so very early in the morning. I was not a morning person. Very soon after my prayer, someone came for me. This was another test. Then I was wheeled down the hallway and parked outside of another room. I waited alone for the scan to be done. A CT scan had been ordered. I remember dreading the idea of getting inside of that machine, which looked like a casket. I didn't want to have to get into that thing.

I sat there alone in the wheelchair, all bundled up with a warm blanket, waiting. I watched nurses and doctors walk by me. They would smile and go about their business. I did overhear one conversation about how they were planning their evening. Pity tried to come onto me. I did wonder, *Why me?* Something way down deep on the inside of me thought that God must be up to something. I just could not accept the idea of dying. I did not believe for one millisecond that it was my time to go. I just prayed all of these prayers, wanting and desiring to know God. I was not trying to hear Him through another human being. I wanted to know my purpose. What was my destiny? What was I destined for? What was mine? My life had not even begun yet. I could not leave yet. My life was a mess. My house was not in order. That was not the time for me to depart. And boy, this was the biggest concern— to stand before Him, not having the chance to answer the call. I was just heading in that direction. Then boom. I was hit, knocked out in the fight. It felt like it came out of nowhere until I remembered how I had been expecting bad news.

So there I was—more sitting and more waiting. Something that I had not experienced before began to happen to me. I began shaking uncontrollably. I thought something was wrong with me again. It was not my nerves. I got colder and colder, and I could not seem to get warm. It just felt so very cold. I was already cold from the temperature in that place. This was different. I was shaking and freezing. Then my mouth was shaking to the point of my teeth chattering. Tears began to flow. It felt like streams of living waters. I could not hold them back as hard as I tried. They kept coming.

I was wheeled inside of the room. It was time for the scan. Getting inside of the machine was not as frightening to me anymore. I lay there in what looked like the dead man's casket. It did not close shut all the way. If it had, I might not have gotten in it. Now the shaking was more intense. It felt like my entire being was vibrating with electricity. I was not frightened by this. I was at peace. There He was! I could see Him in the vision. I saw what I believed to be Jesus. It was so very plain to me. There's no confusion about it. I could see a cross and how He was struggling to carry it. It was heavy. I could see how He was all beaten up, bloody, and bruised. A crown of thorns was on His head in the vision that played out before me. I saw a dirty, sandy pathway where He was walking, dragging His cross on His back. It was more than real to me.

It was my truth. He came for me. I do believe that I got to see the Real One. The real Jesus. He spoke to me personally. Again this is what I believe. It was just this tender voice speaking to me. I believed it was Him when I heard Him say to me, "Child, I have healed you. Child, I have healed you. Child, I have healed you." I believe I heard it spoken directly to me three times. Just like that. It was said directly to me, Jennifer. I do not doubt it. I know. He revealed Himself to me. Then I do believe He said to me, "It is done. It is finished." And that was my vision. I share it with you because there is a world of people who need it. They need Jesus.

I was in awe. There are no other words to describe what was taking place. I was not taught about healing. I had never been told that Jesus could heal today. And if someone told me, it did not register in my brain. I was not in the right church at that time. It was not attending a church with faith miracles from the Holy Ghost. They did not believe that way. So this faith inside of me had to come from somewhere. It was not taught where I had been. It just sprang up from within me. It came up from my heart.

Larry had been waiting for me in my room. I was wheeled back there. During the wheelchair ride, I was trying to take it all in. What had just happened to me, and what did that mean for me? But somewhere in the depths of me, I knew. I just needed to tell that reasoning mind of mine to shut up.

I began trying to explain it to Larry. But I could tell by the blank look on his face that he did not know what I was talking about. I did not think that he believed me. I wanted him to believe me so that I would feel safe enough to believe it myself. I did not know any better at that time. But he had no experience with spiritual manifestations of the Holy Ghost. He had not heard or been taught … until now! There is a first time for everything. He thought the medications were beginning to get to me. He even called one of my nurses to get me something to help calm me down. I waited there in that hospital bed with major anticipation. I was excited. I was expecting. Larry was just going to have to see for himself just like those male disciples did. A woman came yelling and shouting. "He is risen!" Ha-ha! He got up from that grave! Hallelujah! And I was about to *get up* from my own! I'd had enough death and gloom already. It was time to *live* ... and live well.

One of my doctors came to my room. She ordered the staff to take me back downstairs again. But this time she wanted an ultrasound done because of the test results. It came back. *The doctors could not find the blood clot. It had disappeared.* Just as I heard those words, I leaped up from that bed with a shout of joy! I knew it! It was true! There was no doubt about it. Larry looked at me, almost in disbelief. It was shocking news. But it was very good news—news that I would not ever forget. I had been given a dawn of new hope! I felt a gladness and a joy that I had not known before. I felt honored (see Esther 8:16). I truly believed that I had seen the light!

The lady who was running the ultrasound machine did not see anything. I remember the smile on my face. I felt like I was glowing. My God really loved me. I was a special case after all. I viewed myself as God's special case from that day on. I had received my very own healer. That was what I believed, and nobody was going to change my mind about that. I was very blessed and highly favored by God Himself. The medical doctors had no answer for me. They were speechless really. They looked totally baffled, and they even apologized for the mishap. I had the answer that I needed. And I was going to go and to tell others.

Before I was released to go home, a nurse came to my room. I do not remember seeing this one before. She had heard about my news, namely that I received a healing miracle! She was a believer as well. She looked at me and told me that God had something very special for me to do for Him, that there was a purpose to my life. To me, that was better news than winning the lottery.

I got to go home. I was free from taking any medications and free from injections in my abdomen. And I was able to throw out that diet plan! I had such peace in my heart. I experienced a type of love that I had yearned for. I was still in awe and completely thrilled by how God had shown up for me, Jennifer. I sat on the bench, waiting for Larry to drive up with the car. The sun was out and shining brightly right on me! But we were not in sunshiny Florida. We had moved off to the state of Georgia. I do recall sitting there, feeling the warmth on my face. I made a promise to God right there. I told Him that I would go and tell the world of what He had done for me.

Now I did not ever dream of writing a book. That idea had never cross my mind. I pictured myself holding a little piece of paper with some notes written out on it, going around to churches, telling the people of this healer I had met personally. I did even try just that. Not all wanted to hear what I had to say about Him. Some of the people I thought would be thrilled no longer looked at me in the same way as before. I felt more and more like an outcast. But that was not going to stop me. I attended my first speaking engagement with my paper in hand just as I had pictured it. It was a nice opportunity. This pastor told me that only one other man than himself had ever stood up in front of his weekly night Bible study. And it had been years since that man had been allowed to do so. No woman had ever gone where Jennifer got to go that evening. She went behind that pastor's pulpit. He even offered to film her story and send it out to see what would happen. But that did not sit right with me. He did not want to put me up in front of his congregation. He was afraid of the outcome. Those big tithes would stop. Certain men would think that the pastor was allowing a woman to preach to them! They would get up and walk out. He was honest with me, and I respected him for that. Waiting to see what may happen does not speak faith to me. That is not faith, not my kind of faith. I believed that God had me leave there. That was not my place. And we said our good-byes and left in peace. It hurt, and I had to deal with feeling rejected. I did not leave there with a bad attitude. I wasn't going to slander the man of God. That was not my heart at all. I did not agree with everything there. It was not for me, and I knew it.

I was asked to do an interview for some broadcast on the Internet. I do not even know what became of that. It was not something that I naturally wanted to do. I sat there in fear without any paper. No notes. It was way out of my comfort zone for sure. I had to get the camera crew to move the camera out from my face. It made me too nervous. I was not comfortable with that little setup at all. My flesh dreaded it. They were asking questions, but there was no preparing for this. I just had to go and do it. I was not told ahead of time what they would ask me. I did not get to prepare what I would say. I had no idea about what I was going to say. I got through it. Just as I was beginning to relax and enjoy myself, then it was over.

Another filming invitation came too. Oh, I hated the cameras. They often make you look much heavier than what you actually are. And they just made me very uncomfortable. I did not like them. I was able to write out on a large poster board all that I had to say. I made it through the filming, and it was later shown to a congregation.

The next invite was even more intense for me. I had to get up in front of people on the platform with microphone in hand. No paper, no notes. Someone was going to ask questions to help me through the event, but I still didn't know what the questions would be. I believed that God was going to show up and to help me. If not, then I was doomed. I was facing my fears. And it was not easy for me, but in the end, it was very satisfying.

We have been told not to despise the small beginnings. Even when God calls us out to open our homes and to minister to one other person, that is still significant to God. There is a life involved.

When my daughter Hope was in middle school, we had a little get-together that was intended to be a Bible study in our home. It was once a week after school. The girls would come home with Hope and some would show up later. I do wonder if they remember how I had them huddled in a circle with their swords drawn—the ladies, the female warriors of God! Now I had no training whatsoever for this. I did not know how to lead a group of girls in middle school. The laughing and the noise that is so typical of that age group was not easy to compete with. Their phones were constantly going off. I finally spoke up and told them that I was not about to even try to compete with all of that. They could choose to shut them down and listen to me or just have at it. And then I would be done. I certainly was not going to force them to hear what I had to say. I did not even know what to say during those meetings. I was just relying on God to help me. And He did. The girls chose me over the phones. It was a miracle. They were respectful, and each one participated in our group discussion time. It was just a time to answer their questions and to love them right where they were. I loved all of them, especially my own daughter. That was our little group. I named it "Daughter's with Destinies." I had no idea what I had gotten myself into. I did not feel qualified. I just stepped out and followed my heart.

Bye-Bye, Louis

"For there is nothing trustworthy or steadfast or truthful in their talk; their heart is destruction or a destructive chasm, a yawning gulf; their throat is an open sepulcher; they flatter and make smooth with their tongue" (Psalm 5:9 AMP). My God is the God of truth. There is no lie in Him. He tells the truth. Even when we may not want to hear it, he is still truthful.

According to the Word of God, He will destroy those who speak lies. The Lord abhors and rejects the bloodthirsty and deceitful men (see Psalm 5:6 AB). Some just refuse God and choose to rebel against Him. If they ever ask God to forgive their actions and sinful hearts, then of course, God will show mercy, for He is a God of mercy. He forgives continually. He does not refuse a true and humbled heart.

The more I come to know about God and His true nature, the more in awe of Him I am. He still amazes me. He is a God of justice. He does pay us back for all the wrong that has been done to us. I see how much better it is to forgive our enemies and to bless them in prayer. We then get released and set free from the offense. Then we allow God to deal with them. Rather than us trying to get revenge, it is far better to drop it and to forgive and leave the matter in God's hands. God does repay.

I had major trust issues. I put my trust in some I had no business trusting. I trusted too soon. And there were those I once trusted in because I was a child, and that is what children do. They believe what they are told whether it is really true or not. It is truth to them. The breath of the Almighty began to give me understanding (see Job 32:8). And I still praise Him for truth. I love truth. I fight for truth. I refuse to live a lie. I hate lies. You can love people but hate the deceit that is operating inside of them. I hate the Devil, and I hate what he stands for. He constantly opposes God. He attacks God's people. The time is coming—and it is coming very soon—when he will be locked down and put away for a period of time. Then he gets out again for a second round, but then again he gets moved out of the way—forever. Hallelujah! So in the meantime, we get to deal with him and his constant scheming and lies. He uses people and deceives them. I cannot think of anyone who would willingly say, "Come on in, Devil, and use me." Maybe some do. I do not know.

I want no part of him. And the more and more that I have come to know about my God, the less the Devil has to use against me. He is a trickster. And he did really have me fooled—more times than I would have preferred. But he did not get away with it. Truth did come out, for it always does. The light exposed him. Some people thought they would fool the Holy Spirit with their lying and covering up. Think again! One may be so duped and try to even fool themselves along with others. But you are not going to get away with trying to lie and trying to fool God. The deceitfulness may work for a time, but eventually, it will be exposed one way or another.

My God has put more rejoicing inside of my heart, more so than they know (see Psalm 4:7). God has received my prayers time and time again. He has remained faithful to me. He has always come through for me regardless of the wait time involved. Some things took longer than others. I'm still waiting on some things. I am choosing to allow patience to work inside of me. Patience builds character. I know that God has given me gifts directly. It is going to require much character to stay on this journey of mine.

Faith and patience go hand in hand. One cannot have one without the other. I have heard it said that you have as much faith as you do patience! Selah! Pause and think of that. Before I understood this principle I would try to dismiss certain things from my heart because I did not know the truth about them. I did not see results right away, and I would just want to forget about certain things. But God would bring these back up to my heart. He would not allow me to forget about them. I was constantly seeking Him. He knew how serious I was to have His truth in this matter. He was faithful to me in showing me His truth, not some man or woman's made-up truth.

Deep calls to deep. It is all about how deep one's desires go. "But let all those who take refuge and put their trust in You rejoice; let them sing and shout for joy, because You make a covering over them and defend them; let those also who love Your name be joyful in You and be in high spirits" (Psalm 5:11 AB). I love His name—Jesus. He comforts me and soothes this soul of mine. He is the lifter of my head (see Psalm 3:3 AB). I so rejoice in this truth. God has literally lifted up my head and caused me to straighten up my back and shoulders. He has caused me to walk a new walk. I no longer want to hide.

I have become. And I am becoming. I am coming out! Hallelujah! Just like the song goes. Praise God. I refuse to walk around with a false sense of humility. I did that. It was misery to. There was no life and peace. It was religion, a false religion. I did not know any better. I allowed myself to feel bad, for I did not know any other way to live. I was a believing Christian, and I believed something that was not true. I liked nice things. I admired those who had them, those who looked all pretty and put together with the nice bling on their hands and arms. I was attracted to really nice stuff. Quality was far better than quantity to me.

There was such a stronghold in my head about that materialism. But my heart wanted to believe different. It did not make any sense to me. I was willing to walk away from it all. I would have given it all.

As much as I liked all of the stuff, it did not have the power to love me back. There was no power in any of it to strengthen me. It may have put a smile on my face, but it did not cause that spiritual glow. I was ridiculed time and time again. Shame played inside of me, and it came out through other people. They were being used by the Devil. They were actually victims themselves.

There was no way in this world that some handbag or some high-dollar item was going to give me what I really desired. It just was not going to come through a material item. I tried that path, not even realizing what I was doing at the time. It did not work. I wanted my stuff. Let's get that straight. But if it came down to choosing between the stuff or God, then I knew exactly what I would do. I chose Him. I did give it all away only to discover that I already had what I was searching for. God did not require me to go out. I had been duped into doing all that. I was deceived. I needed to be delivered from the wrong teachings that played over and over inside of my head. I was in desperate need of a mind renewal. I desired to glow in the glory of God. No handbag or no worldly possession was going to bring that about.

The very first high-end bag that I received was so very special to me. There was more to it than just receiving the bag. Many will tell you that Christians should not waste their money on such high-dollar items. It is wasteful, and all of that money spent on a bag could go toward helping someone else. Others will say that having such luxurious items will hurt one's ministry. Where do people come up with these ideas? These are just ideas that someone has turned into what they think is the truth. And then it is pushed onto to a person in an attempt to make other people feel guilty. Or better yet, there is something wrong with you. Some say, "Oh, I would not ever spend that kind of money on a handbag. I'd feed starving children before I went and did that." How do you know the one spending the money on the bag is not doing just that and more? People are so quick to judge and do not even know what goes on behind closed doors, let alone what is in the heart of other people who just so happen to enjoy certain possessions. I have known some with no interest in luxury items or lifestyles. That type of living is not for everyone. Not all would consider that enjoyable. Some rather be up in the mountains in a sleeping bag or out hunting and trying to shoot innocent deer. I do not like that! I have a heart for animals, especially ones with fur. Maybe for you it is your Harley and the leather with fringe flying from your boots. It is one thing not to have any desire for the finer things in life but another to judge those who do want these things. And just because I happen to enjoy the finer lifestyle, that does not mean that I do not enjoy other things as well—drinking a cup of good coffee, sitting on the beach and enjoying the sunshine, wearing a sundress with a large straw hat, walking around with my little Chihuahua, Romeo. He is very entertaining. In his little mind, his entire mission in life is to protect me. He tries to be my bodyguard. If anyone should stare at me for too long or someone he does not approve of tries to approach me, he rises up like a lion. I do enjoy the spa, and depending on where you go, that might not be a simple thing. I enjoy my manicures and pedicures. I like looking down and seeing well-kept toes. And there is not any earthly thing better than seeing your children smile, knowing they are at peace, confident and authentic children of God.

A simple kiss from your spouse. A hug when it is needed. A lunch date with a dear friend. Girl time. A drive beneath the stars. Listening to a song that moves you and touches your heart. Enjoying the quietness and stillness of your soul. Being a lady at rest. Enjoying home life. The satisfaction of knowing who you are and what you stand for. I could keep going. There is much more to me than liking fine clothes, high-end jewels, and designer handbags.

It took me working up some courage to ever walk into the store where that high-end bag sat. I was in the later part of my twenties. I wanted to go inside and to see. I was curious. I knew some would not approve. I already could imagine what some would say, and I could visualize their facial expressions. I was not even going to set myself up for that. No way. I was learning about what the Bible referred to as "to leave and to cleave." Larry and I were one. We did not need anyone else trying to run our personal lives or marriage. I went home and told Larry about my desire to have that bag, the one that I had had my eye on. It sat inside its own glass case like some precious jewel. That was how I viewed that bag at that time. I warned Larry about the cost before I took him to the store. So he knew beforehand what he was getting into. I made sure that he knew. I wanted to know that it really was okay and not a bad thing to own a high-end bag. It was just something that I desired.

I would go to God with my desires. I wanted to get His okay. I wanted His approval. I would ask of Him to remove the desire for things I was not sure about—*if* it was not of Him. It was a constant struggle to believe that God was okay with materialism, owning expensive stuff. Camping out in the Winnebago was not my thing. I didn't want to sit around the campfire with bugs and critters and snakes and wolves or bears possibly showing up. That was not me.

During many of those times when I went to God, I had really expected Him to take away some of these desires of mine. I had been made to feel so bad about many of them. I felt bad about myself for desiring them in the first place. It was supposed to be wrong. Wrong, wrong, wrong. But I cannot deny the something down in my heart was telling me something different. If only I could just do right, then I could feel right about me. I was in a works mentality. It was all about me performing and doing right. I hated performing. I did not like acting, and I did not think I was very good at it. I did not want to be an actress. I did not even like getting out in front of those lights and cameras, especially when they were right up in front of my face.

You do not work your way into heaven. And you certainly do not buy your ticket there either. Nor does one work your way into being right. People like that are so focused on themselves that they cannot even see God. Their entire focus is on themselves. Then there are the ones who feel so low and insecure. They carry around a false belief system. These people are still constantly focused on themselves. All they think is wrong. They have a false sense of humility. They think it is right. Those types of people think that it pleases God when they act that way. But it does not please Him at all. It is a lie. People like that are suffering from an identity crisis. They do not know who they are. Instead of being able to worship God for who He really is and all that He has already done and provided for you, you are focused only on yourself, focusing on all that is wrong with you. You are continually worshipping yourself then. How can people like that truly worship their maker when they cannot seem to get their hearts and minds off from themselves? What is your primary focus on? Or who? You or Him? This life with God is not about one feeling right about him or herself. It is all about receiving. It is about being made right and knowing you have been made right and alive to Christ. It has nothing to do with you working to obtain what all Christ has freely made available to you. Believe and receive. It sounds so simple.

In the very same year, life just took off like a rocket ship for Larry and me. I got my dream house up on the hill. I got the Mercedes, and I did get the bag. And it also came with a wallet full of cash I could spend. It was not wishful thinking that brought me the positive results into my life. And it certainly had nothing to do with luck. It had everything to do with my belief system, which had taken a turn in a far better direction.

I got to spend my thirtieth birthday in a home that had once been only a dream. It seemed impossible to even get a house like that! Larry and I had believed, and our business took off. It did not happen overnight. It took diligence day after day, night after night. I was determined to see it happen. And I did not want to keep depending on my grandfather for financial help. Yes, Papa did come back into the picture, and he gave us some money. When we moved to Georgia, he helped us. Larry walked away from all that he had known. The old life that he had lived was now over. Georgia was a new beginning in a new location. Larry choosing to work for another company was not the most comfortable thing either. Once you have been self-employed and you are used to running the show and being your own boss, having to go back to a job with a new boss is not a desirable thing. I sure would not want to do it. I did not want another person telling me what to do. Punching a time card was not for me.

Being fired from a job can be humiliating for a man. But it can turn into a great blessing. I saw it as an answer to our prayers. I danced around the house like a happy white woman. I set up shop for him in the little dining room that we had at that time. I was in a great praise mode. I saw the job as a major hindrance to us. It was not the vision. The business was the vision, and I was ready for it to come to pass. I saw skyscrapers. I could see unlimited possibilities. My heart was beginning to soar just like the eagle. I was alone in all that I really believed, but it no longer mattered. Larry was catching on. I got to believe and seek God, and Larry got to do the work part. I was beginning to really like our partnership!

All that I could see did not match up to the way we were living, but it gave me hope. Being able to see—and see it well—was fabulous to me. It was glorious and quite grand. More scales were coming off my eyes. There was no stopping this dreaming heart of mine. It was thrilling to know that I could turn to God and that He would hear me and answer me. I trusted that He would send me my answers and that He would give me what I asked Him for. That amazed me. I liked Him more and more. I needed Him. There was nobody else out there like Him. He was a keeper for sure.

I was learning to look to God as I did my papa. I just did not get the unconditional love part yet. That was still to come. Papa had become like a father to Larry. Larry never had anyone help him out like that before. It showed Larry a side to God that he had not known. It was well needed.

So we lived in this little rental house in Georgia, and we started the business from that dining room. It seemed like an eternity to get that thing up and going. I was so certain that it would work. In fact, I was not taking no for an answer. I just knew that we had to go for it and not quit. Prayer and determination and speaking out life over what we wanted to see happen paid off. The thrill of the first job made all of the waiting time worth it. It was worth it. I was so thankful. I did not go from A to B to C. This little rental was nothing compared to the house I believed we would get. We would take a drive up that hill time and time again. I could see myself moving into that neighborhood. Larry liked it too. He just did not understand what I was thinking. He told me so over and over again. But he was always willing to take the drive up the hill with me. He would say, "I do not know what you are smoking, but I am willing to believe with you." I was not smoking anything. I had never smoked a cigarette or a joint. That was not for me. I had no interest in that.

Getting that house was a God thing. There is no other answer for it. My God worked out the details for me so that I could have it. I believed Him regardless of the circumstances, and He came through for me. I was dancing with joy. He was revealing more and more of Himself to me. And He was doing so in the natural world with natural things to show me the spiritual side of life. I enjoyed Him more and more. I was learning that He was nothing like the way I once viewed Him. The picture of Him that others had painted for me was perfectly wrong. That was not Him at all.

I went through different styles of handbags and went through different homes in different places there in Georgia. We had moved on from my house on the hill. (Later on, I would really miss it.) One house that I thought I absolutely had to have turned into one bad dream. We were there six months, and we had not sold our prior house yet. So there we were with two huge houses and two large mortgage payments. The room off the kitchen was always so cold. It had a beautiful fireplace, but I never could get warm in there. I did not care so much for the house. It was large with beautiful furnishings all throughout. Hope had her own master suite with her own master bathroom upstairs. This little princess had her very own garden tub. My son had quite the room for himself too. He had a large television of his own, a sofa, an oversized chair, and a coffee table. It was not a tight space either. He still had plenty of space to walk around in. And he had a king-size bed. He lived in there like a little king. My master suite was downstairs. So we were all spread out and apart. It looked really pretty, but it was the worst thing at that particular time for our family. My son began having problems in the local school. This arrangement was not working out so very well. I sat before the Lord one morning. I needed an answer. The response did not surprise me. I was already sensing it. But now I had to tell Larry. I really thought he would think I had lost my mind. I prayed before approaching him. I needed help. I needed favor from God. I believed the Lord instructed me to move back to the other house. It was not quite as nice as this one, and the layout of it was completely different. It was not as grand to me. The style was different. They were both nice, just very different. Both were brand new. All of them had been new except the rental. That one did not count. We were only renting. I've always preferred brand new. There is just something about new things that I like. Now I would also take a fixer-upper gladly and make it new. I would enjoy that. I like character. It would be fun to find the right older home that had my style and rip it apart and make it my own. I do think that could be very enjoyable. I like renovations, especially with homes, including my own house.

I did what I had to do. It did not feel comfortable. I felt like Esther! I had to chose to be obedient and go before the king of my house. I did not have an entire year of beauty treatments to look my best and to smell my best either. That may have been very nice—an entire year at the spa day after day. I would not have lasted. I would have gotten bored and would have been out of there. Anyway, it was a good thing, a very favorable thing that my king found me rather attractive and one of real beauty!

Okay, I am stopping right here. Larry has no idea that I am referring to him as the king of my home. So Larry, when you read this, do not let this go to your head! I cannot even believe that I am typing this out. And most likely, I will not say or write it ever again. I do love you, but you know that this is not my style. I have one King, and you know who He is. There is one King to my heart, and His name is Jesus.

So off I went down in the basement of our castle, the one we were being called to leave. I stood there. He looked up from his desk with a pleasant look on his face, waiting for me to speak to him. "What is it, Jennifer?" he said. So I spoke. I told him about my news. I believed that we needed to leave. I already had God's favor. I am glad that I did not need to fast three days before approaching my king! I just had to go and do what I believed God said for me to do.

I already had won Larry's heart. I did not even need to try. He just fell for me. He loved me because he wanted to. He chose to. Or maybe at times he did not feel love for me. Perhaps during some of those undesirable times, he was too hurt by me or frustrated at me to feel anything. But he never left. He did not stray. He chose me over and over again. He was not going anywhere, but rather he was going along with me. I had much favor indeed.

Telling him was not an easy thing to do. I was still trying to get over how crazy it sounded. And all the money that we had shelled out by moving in there was not going to just jump back into our checking account. Larry did look at me the way I had anticipated. I knew him well enough to know in advance that God would have to deal with his heart in this matter. It did not matter how much of a beauty queen Larry thought I was. This instruction sounded ludicrous. I did what I was called to do. Queen Jennifer made her royal appearance and did what she needed to do. Then she departed. Her part was now over. It was now between Larry and God. I was off the hook. I went back up into the house, my little castle.

Larry had our guys working down in the basement, decking out his new office. It was wintertime and cold out. The business was slow for a short period of time. We paid the guys to work at the house. And now we were called to leave before Larry's office was finished. He had dreamed of an office like that. And now he would not even get to enjoy it. Sorry, love. I laugh at this little story now. I think of how foolish I was, racing off to buy the thing in the first place.

King Larry came upstairs to greet me rather quickly. God had done a very quick work. He agreed that we should go back. So we did. We had more furniture than we knew what to do with. We got rid of what we did not need. A neighbor across the street yelled out to me, "Did you have yourself a nice vacation?" I can only imagine what the neighbors were saying. The most important thing to me was obeying God, regardless of what anyone had to say about the things that I did.

I still struggled with this handbag issue. It was so tormenting. I would make progress and go forward only to find myself being pulled back into misery and doubt over it. I would try to figure out if it was okay or not. I thought I had it settled, and then it would come creeping back up on me, bringing confusion with it. That should have been a red flag right there. It just did not make any sense to me. But it tormented me. I was tormented by these thoughts. I needed deliverance. I needed to bring the past things that nobody wanted to talk about out into the open. It was causing me to suffer health problems too. I even had a doctor that apparently God gave me favor with well God seemed to have given me favor with just about all of them. And there were many. But this one took time out of his day and sat there with me for more than an hour. He had a heart filled with compassion for me. He asked me personal but appropriate questions that might pinpoint some of those undesirable symptoms. He began talking to me about traumas. I couldn't understand what he meant at the time, but I see now. And I now understand what he was trying to say to me. He wanted to help me but couldn't. I could not even help myself. I still had no remembrance. I could only see a portion of it in my head. I still was not able to see what had really taken place. The trauma was on the verge of making itself known. It could not stay buried in me forever.

I said good-bye to the high-end bag. I gave it away to a woman I had become close with. I was still living with that shameful nature and a false sense of humility. I didn't know who I was or what my real identity was either. I had God. There was no doubt about that. And His power was operative in my life. But I was lacking much truth. Thinking something and knowing a truth are very different things. Reasoning is not knowing. And knowledge has nothing to do with real faith. I gave the handbag away with fear in my heart. I was not going to allow some handbag to stop me or prevent me from going further into the things of God. I believed that He had too much in store for me to let a bag get in the way. I was all wrapped up in emotions. Larry just said to me that I'd better make sure that I am really hearing God because he wasn't going to get me another one. He was not joking when he said that either. I had felt so good about my choice. I thought that I was doing the right Christian thing, giving it away to a person who did have the means to buy one for herself. It sounded so good. But a good thing is not always a God thing! I learned that lesson over and over again the hard way.

I remember the day when I drove off down the road to deliver my goods. I had wrapped it up all nice and tidy in its original bag. And I had hand-written a nice letter to. I released the bag. I felt like I had done the right thing.

Until the very next day! I did not have any other high-end bag to use. I had already given those out to other people. But I had given those with a different heart. I did not want them to just sit on the shelf in my closet, collecting dust. I was getting new ones, so I got rid of the old. I was not into changing out bags on a daily basis. I did not have time or the patience for that back then.

My emotions wore off rather quickly, and I was beginning to regret the choice I had made. It was just like buying that house. It did not take long before I no longer wanted that house. I remember sitting in my car inside the garage and crying. My papa was no longer here and available to help me. He had already lived out his life here and had kept his promise to me. He always would tell me how he thought that he had been put here to make sure that I would be taken care of and be cared for. God willing, he was not going anywhere until he knew that I would be okay. My papa made it clear to me that he felt his purpose in life was looking after me. Papa helped me feel somewhat special. He did try his hardest to treat me like a little princess. And I did thoroughly enjoy the attention my papa gave to me time and time again. I noticed the many times he and other people would talk, but whenever I came into the room, he would always acknowledge me. He would pay attention to me regardless of who was there. Papa would make sure that he noticed me. He'd make the royal announcement. "Here comes my good-looking granddaughter." Papa really thought that I was something grand. He saw something in me that I could not see for myself. In his own way, he did give me a cloak of many colors to wear. A prophet once told me that I had my own female version of the Joseph story. Now there's a thought. Papa believed that I would help other people someday. As a child, I never quite knew what he meant by that, but it sounded rather delightful. It sounded like it could be very true.

I remember God saying to me, "You cannot just go and return a house like you can go and return a pair of shoes!" My faith caused me to believe that God could do anything. I wanted Him to get me out from the mess I had gotten myself into with that house. Wax on, wax off! I put the wax on, but now I wanted someone else come get it off for me!

Now my handbag was gone. I went to the store and looked for a cheap regular bag. I quickly started regretting what I had done. Larry already told me that we were not purchasing any more bags. I walked around for a week without a purse. I put my personal belongings in a plastic ziplock bag and left it sitting inside of my Mercedes. I did have a conversation with God about this handbag situation *again*. He knew my heart, and He knew why I did what I did. I believe that God dealt with Larry's heart in the matter. And then our business got another job—one that Larry had not been expecting. It came at just the right time. I just kept coming back to the same place with the same answer. There was nothing wrong with being a Christian, a born-again lady filled with the Holy Ghost, and carrying around a high-end bag.

I kept trying to tell this to a woman who was in my life. I kept telling her that I did not agree with her as nicely as I could. I would share with her what I believed God was showing me. It just was not going over so well. I had a choice. I could listen to her or do what my heart was trying to tell me to do. I could not always hear right until I got away from the other voices trying to speak to me. And some people are not going to sit there and be quiet. They think they know better, and they are going to make themselves heard one way or another. I had to get away from that disapproval. I could not take it anymore. If I did not agree and act in all of the way's this person expected of me, then she disapproved of me. And there was much more expectation than putting away a handbag. I loved her, and she loved me. But this was an unhealthy relationship. It brought me to an awful point, a point of no return. She was not willing to go with me. I did not know her real heart. But I did know that she was holding me back from becoming the woman I wanted to become.

I was desperate to move forward in the right direction. To go where I desired, I could not remain close to her. I let go. It was time to let go. I flapped my wings and realized I could fly. I just needed to fly alone for a time. I could not go free and follow God in the course that He wanted to take me if I kept in contact with this person. It was too conflicting and confusing. It was difficult to *fly* away, but I did. And God was with me.

I would allow myself to get attached very easily to certain women with motherly tendencies. I would set myself up to get hurt over and over again, not realizing what I was doing. I did finally get my boundaries straightened out. I recognized that the problem was inside of me. Once I had dealt with this issue and healed, the types of people I hung around changed. I was no longer attracted to the same types. And I no longer just sat back and allowed any person to come into my life and attach themselves to me. I got free from playing the rescuer as well. I also got free from the false sense of responsibility for another's actions. That was huge for me! I was not going to live as an enabler. I was once very unhealthy inside, and it attracted other unhealthy people. I wanted to be alone with God so that He could change me. I no longer wanted to keep going around in circles in the same type of situations just with different people. And that was what I set out to do. I got away from all of them. It was me, Larry, my children, and my God. And I was fine with it.

Larry had a change of heart, and he bought me another high-end bag. I got three in total with a new wallet. It was a larger one, and it would hold more cash. And I did have a nice smile on my face too. And I had a heart that wanted to know God more and more.

The blind cannot lead the blind, for they both eventually fall into a ditch. I was tired of the ditches. And I was tired of being used. I played the rescuer role with far too many people, trying to rescue them and make it easier for them. It was a way to feel needed and to feel important. All for a good cause, I thought. I thought I was doing the right thing, the Christian thing. I learned some pretty hard life lessons. It had become exhausting and too stressful. It was downright painful.

Giving away the high-end bag was one thing. I gave it away because I was duped and deceived. But then it did not stop there. It started with that and ended with me giving away my entire house of new furnishings. The house was almost completely empty. And I remember Hope asking me not to give away anything that was in her room. She was a preteen, but somehow she knew better.

Larry was in on this with me. I certainly did not have the house emptied out while he was away. I was known back then to write out checks and send out to ministries. I had the Christian stations going 24-7. I was sowing our seed. Larry would come home, concerned with how much I had given away today. I was in a season of constantly giving high dollar amounts. And I thought I was doing what I was supposed to be doing. I heard of stories where God told people to get rid of their possessions. Then something wonderful would happen for them. I do not know why God asks certain people to do certain things. It is between God and that individual. I do know in the Christian world we are called to live by our faith. Some have more faith than others. And a person can believe one thing, but it does not mean they have faith in another particular area.

Just because God tells one person to do something like giving any all of his possessions, that does not mean He's saying that to the entire world. What God may speak to me to do, He may not speak to you. Every believer is called to live the Christian life. We are called to allow His Spirit to lead us. The Holy Spirit is not going to call you out of sinful ways. If you are a believer and are stuck like glue in a situation you know you shouldn't be in, God will help you. He will be faithful to you if you want Him to be.

I did not get some large check delivered to me in the mail with God's signature on it. It did not work that way. And it was not due to my lack of faith either. I could believe many things, things that seemed very unnatural to the human mind. For me, it seemed so easy. I have discovered that I was given the gift of faith. It comes so natural to me to believe in things that others do not have the faith for. There wasn't a pot of gold sitting out in my backyard or a massive explosion of money falling from the sky.

I sat there in that empty house, staring at blank walls for more than a year. I must say that it was rather depressing. I had my moments of joy, but I did not know how to keep them. And it was not just because the furniture was gone. The professionally made drapes were gone. The fine china and the cabinet it once sat in so beautifully were gone too. I had once had beautiful hanging mirrors and wall portraits. My favorite thing of all was a pretty green, round, tufted ottoman. I gave away my son's king-size bed and furnishings. The house furnishings were wiped out. I even paid to have it all hauled away. We still had the plantation shutters hanging up. I am surprised that we did not take those down and send them off too. Those emotions of mine sure did play me for a fool. I was sad. I thought that I had heard God. I thought what I had done had been all for God. I thought I was being led by Him and by His Spirit inside of me. Or so I thought. I thought wrong. It was not Him. I had been duped.

God, Where Are You?

Was any of this You? The giving away of all of the stuff was not what upset me so badly. I knew how to believe God. That was how I got the stuff to begin with. I had faith. Good faith that worked out right for me. It was the being duped and the deception that had been at play. Things can be replaced, even if there's a time involved in waiting. My heart was another matter altogether.

It was one problem or one hurt right after another in some of these Christian circles. It appeared I did better out in the heathen world. Not that I was about to ever go walking away from God. That was not my heart at all. Nor was I ever going back to that old way of life. That was not living at all. Some of this stuff that these Christian people came up with—and that I fell for—really made me stop and ask, "God, is this really You?"

It really felt to me that I was in the middle of a tug-of-war. God was at one end, and the Devil was at the other end. Of course, I was in the middle. My fire temporarily blew out of me while I was seeking truth. I was not in a good mental place to be out running all over and screaming from the rooftops. It was time for resting and seeking Him out like never before. It was difficult because I was hurting. I did not understand how in the world God allowed me to get into some of the situations I found myself in. And I believed at that time that God was in control of everything that happened to a person, that He was using these situations to teach lessons for a higher cause and purpose, specifically to mold me. I learned how to run to God with my wounds from other people. But what do you do when you feel so wounded by God Himself?

I lay in my bed one night and even asked Him, "How could you let this happen to me?" I blamed Him. I did not know better. I was confused. I was the type of person who wanted figure it all out. I have been known to be a very deep thinker. I wanted answers. I had so many questions. My ultimate purpose in this life was to know God. That was the prayer and concern of my own very heart—*to know Him.* I was not able to throw out a bunch of Scripture passages at people. The Paul I read of in the Bible said that wasn't his desire. Paul said he wanted to know God. I have come to greatly appreciate God's written Word. Heaven knew how badly I needed them. There is life and power in those words—enough life and power to change one's life.

I have had faith that could move mountains. Again, just because people have faith for one thing does not mean that they have it for another. I have gotten very carried away in the faith department. Now I realize some of those times were not faith at all. It was saying, "Let's try this and see if it works." Faith is knowing beforehand. It is certainty. I got into situations that I would have never asked to have been in. And I no longer believe that God asked me or called me to be in some of those messes either.

The tug-of-war was at hand. There are many voices going on in this world. I know that God is speaking. He will speak to His children. And I do know the Devil is talking too. And I am not referring to loud audible voices, although God did talk through a donkey. There is a story in the Bible about a man who would not listen. God was trying to get his attention. So the donkey spoke for real. Now can you picture the look on the man's face? My goodness. I have thought that it would be nice to have my little Chihuahua start talking to me. I can see it now. "Mummy, God said you need to do this!" Okay, that would be a little crazy ... and probably make the headline news. "Little black Chihuahua speaks out for the first time."

I never dreamed of Satan coming through certain people. And I believe that some of those people were just as duped as I was. I also know of one who seemed to be employed by Satan himself, given the scheming and lying. That individual was very bloodthirsty. She did not want to leave me alone. I did not understand it. But I sure do get it now. While the tug-of-war was going on with me, I was actually saying, "Get behind me, Satan," when it was God and not the Devil. At times I was deceived, and I thought that the Devil was actually God speaking to me. We live in a spiritual world. I did not realize what I was doing. The Devil dupes. He deceives. How else can he get people to listen to him? Once you learn of him and his lying, scheming ways, you no longer have to be his prey. I refused to live out my entire life being some kind of victimized Christian. No way. Not me. I had authority given to me from God Himself. I just had to discover it and find out how to use it. There was power available to me. It scared that Devil to no end. That is why he fought so hard. He did not want me finding it out. Then I could become his worst nightmare.

The Holy Spirit came so many times through my life. I did not know what that was. So many times it could have saved me from so much heartache if I would have paid attention. But I could not. I did not know. *I know now though.* Even though I went against some of those promptings and found myself in a mess, God never left me alone. Wax on, wax off! I have been in numerous dangerous situations. My life was at stake. I know all about being beat up, tossed around, knocked down, kicked in my side, and spat on like I was some sort of piece of trash— and by somebody who claimed to love me. I have had dishes thrown at me and broken all over the place. I've been called very vile names and left to clean up the mess. I know all about what it is climbing into your own bed at night and trying to fall sleep as you grapple with the fear that is tormenting you. Your own pillow is often soaked in your own tears. I could spend an entire day cleaning and straightening up to have it ripped apart and tossed all over by a mad whirlwind at night.

Even Cinderella did not get dragged around on the carpet by her hair. I have seen the holes in the walls and the furniture turned upside down so that it looked like a massive storm had run its course. I suppose it did. I've experienced having hands around my neck and almost choking me to death while silently praying to God that He would accept me into heaven. Then suddenly, the hands would pull away from me. I know all about it. I have witnessed the rage, the anger. I have danced with the Devil himself. And I do not mean Larry. I have seen the affects that the Devil has had on a person. Did I know this at the time? Certainly not. I know now. And I also know how to shut him down!

There is so much more to this Christian life, so much more than filling up a seat on a Sunday morning or whatever day service is held. I had no idea what I was getting myself into. But regardless of all that has happened to me, I am so very thankful that I did get in. It has been one wild ride of a lifetime. I do not regret. I have not lived a boring life—that is for sure.

Some of the very people I once thought I desperately needed were the very ones I needed to let go off and run away from. I was not called to stay and to remain in certain environments all for the sake of walking in love. God gave me the ability to run. And now when He tells me to run, I am going to run. Not in fear but in faith.

The Devil fooled me. What more can I say? I gave it all away to only discover that I already had what I was searching for—love, value, and acceptance. I had nothing to prove. But there was plenty for me to receive. I got into trouble when I thought I was in faith, but I was not really in the faith. I could not have been in real faith when I questioned if God was even in them. That was not faith. I was willing to step out and to find out. And I did. I believed that if I was wrong and if it was not Him, then He would still come for me. He would not turn His back on me. He would still be good to me. I would be okay. I was willing to step out and to see. I wanted to learn, and I did. And I did have real faith. I believed that if I was wrong, then God would use what the enemy had meant for my harm and turn it all around and use it for my good. And He has.

The type of ministry that I once was so drawn to is the very thing I want to stay clear of now. I do not want to ever give the impression that one should sow seeds in order to receive healing. You do not buy a healing. You receive it. Jesus paid a hefty price for me and for you. No amount of money can purchase that. It has already been paid for. So take it. Take it by faith.

There are some traditions that are no longer for me. Then there are also the doctrines of the Devil's teaching. He is so very cunning too. It does not look or sound evil. It is right there in what many call Christian teaching. Yes, but who is teaching it? It may start off sounding just right and then take a turn in a completely opposite direction. It may be that man or woman's truth. But it may actually be the farthest thing away from God's truth. I know now. I have been through it. I have seen it firsthand. I got to endure the pain of it all too. Not by myself, of course. There was a much greater one living inside of me to get me through it. I am so very thankful that I desired my own personal relationship with my God. I am so thankful that He desired me and that He wanted me to know Him too. I am so thankful that I did not rely on a man or woman. It is beneficial to be under the right church authority. It is good to be under the right teaching. It is so good to be gathered together in a corporate setting to worship our maker. But I am so glad that God drew me to Him. I gained a closeness with Him that I could not get any other way than by being alone with Him. It is the best thing that has ever happened to me other than Him saving me. He is the very best thing that has ever happened to me. He is very real.

I was once told that running around to some of those conferences without having a home church could be very dangerous for a person. I now understand. I have seen quite a bit. Not everything is always what it appears to be. I never thought that the enemy would use a Christian thing or Christian person to steal my money. I did not know. I did not imagine that man could do something like that. But he can, and he does. I did not know that the Devil could come into a believing Christian and cause that individual to think he is doing God's work. One may think it is the real Holy Spirit when it is really Satan in disguise. I know for certain that God heals. And He heals today. He is the same yesterday as today and forever. I know for sure that God has real manifestations of Himself. I have had them, so I have experience in that area. And I know the Devil can try to—and does temporarily—get away with duping a person with a false manifestation. The Bible tells all about him coming as a counterfeit. He will never be the real deal. He is a fake! He has to fake everything. He will never be God. He will never be anything like God. He is a fallen angel. He may as well get out his pitchfork and his nasty tail and put it between his legs and go to hell, where he belongs. But he won't go on his own. He is going to keep on with his lying and scheming for as long as he can. But the day is coming for him. Oh, glory hallelujah. That day is a coming.

If you are out there trying to follow the Lord by a feeling or a manifestation, then be careful. You could be headed right into a trap. I took the bait. I know all about it. I asked for outward confirmations and that got me into a world of trouble. I had no clue about what the Devil was capable of doing. I do not want to give him any credit either. Neither do I want to go around with my head buried in the sand, unaware of what he will try to do. I am just so very thankful to God for showing me the truth. And now I know and understand how that Devil operates.

I sat in a place where the man called himself a prophet. It looked right. It sounded right. He asked for a certain amount of money, enough for a nice shopping day. While this prophet was speaking, I felt that I was being asked to give an even larger amount. I felt a manifestation, one trying to confirm that it was really God. I took the bait and thought it must be God. Larry and I argued back and forth in our seats about it. We tried to be as quiet about it as we could. We did not even have that amount available yet in our business checking account. You have to have money set aside in there to pay the workers, cover material costs, and so forth. We had checks on the way. Well, my faith said to me that God would have those checks in our mailbox by the time we got home if He really wanted us to release this amount in seed money. And if God really is behind something, you can trust Him. You hear so much of this. I do know God calls people to give. But I also know that the Devil disguises himself as men asking for seed money too, promising that something will take place for you after you give the amount. Then when that false promise does not happen, the person who dealt out all of that money is oblivious. One like that could very easily get upset with God and question His goodness and His faithfulness. It was not God's fault. He was not the one who was behind those scenes at play. God does not require that of you. It was the Devil in disguise. What better way for the enemy to lead people astray—to get them mad at Jehovah God and then to walk away from Him. They are hurting, confused, deceived, broke, and busted. It's one big mess.

I believe in giving. I am still a giver, but not like before. I believe in sowing and reaping. It has been a continual principle in my life, one that I have been quite happy about. I do believe in planting seed money into God's kingdom. I do believe in tithing. I have had experience with God's faithfulness in this area and know for myself. But I have done some very foolish things. I have also learned some pretty hefty lessons.

I felt much confusion in a particular meeting. It was supposed to be of God. And I do believe that part of it was. There was just some other things going on inside of that place that didn't involve God. I couldn't figure it out. I needed revelation. I needed the real truth. I needed to be able to tests the spirits and to discern what was real and of God and what was false and a counterfeit. I had not even heard of such a thing before. I did not realize that that kind of deception was even out there.

I was oblivious to it. I was naive. And I'm not the only one. When the truth of it all came to me, I was infuriated. I wanted something done about it. But I did not know what to do. I had to choose to forgive. There was no other way out of it for me. I knew better. It was very difficult to forgive myself, and it took some time. I felt so beat down. It was so bad. I really do think that the Devil thought he had me that time. I think that he thought he would get me to walk away from God. I was so hurt. Being hurt by people is one thing. Being hurt and thinking it comes from God is another altogether. I felt so alone. He was there, but I would only allow Him to come so close. I was distant to Him. I knew I needed Him. But I was questioning on who this God really was. I had been so duped. My mind began questioning everything that had happened to me. I wanted to know who was behind every last detail. I was determined to know.

The man had asked for a thousand dollars in seed money. I sat there in my seat, and I felt the need to sow two thousand dollars. That is when Larry and I were squirming in our seats. I was determined to sow it. It was God for crying out loud. We had to obey. That was serious business to me. All of the seed sowers were called down to the front. So we went, even though we had already made our check out for two thousand dollars. The man looked at us and said to Larry, "Sir, you've already made your check out for two thousand, haven't you?" Larry nodded his head with a large grin on his face. I was so mad. He had been fussing with me over the amount. Now that we had been called out and noticed, he did not mind taking all the credit. God is the only one who really knew what was going on inside of our hearts. But let me say this. When we were standing up on that platform for all to see, my flesh wanted to kick that man of mine right off from there. I did not like what I was seeing or sensing. It embarrassed me.

People want to be noticed. They want to be recognized. When you give, it should only be between you and God. It is not something you can show off so that you can feel better about yourself and look so holy standing up in front of others. I know all about being so sold on for Jesus that I was willing to make a fool of myself. I did. And He never asked me to.

I was a prime candidate for being duped. I had a buried past and a shame-based nature. I had no interest in showing off my checkbook. I was desperate to know God and to be totally obedient to Him. I wanted so desperately to please Him. I wanted and needed His protection. I did not purposefully desire to disobey. I so wanted to be covered under the shelter of His wings. I was a real desperate housewife, and I was on a mission.

Another prophet man showed up. He knew things about me. I thought it had to be God. Well, the Devil knows what we have been through too. He has been watching. He has been the cause behind most of these evils. Thankfully, he does not know our hearts.

I was told to give ten thousand dollars this time. Honestly, I liked this man better than the last one. We were not told that we had to give it right then. We sent it out to that ministry later, and much more followed. I must say, however, that by the time we got back home, all of those emotions had calmed down. I was not very certain about sowing that ten thousand dollars in seed. We had responsibilities that we needed to take care of. We couldn't ignore them and bury our heads in the sand. All of this seed money of sowing had nothing to do with our regular tithe. It was considered an offering. The tithe is what already belongs to God. An offering is what one gives above the tithe.

The tug-of-war was still going on. I was trying to discern who was who. This had been going on for quite some time. I remember standing outside that place, and I believe I heard a voice from inside say, "This is not of Me. Just go back to your hotel room." I really did not know what to do. I did not really know what to believe. So I stepped out to find out. I always believed that if I heard incorrectly of if I messed up, God would save me. He would come for me. The evil meant to harm me would be turned around and used for my good. I did believe that.

There was risk involved—the risk of failing, the risk of being wrong. But I was willing to take that risk. I wanted to go to higher places. Higher levels with God bring about higher devils. They want to stop you. But I would not be stopped, not even when I felt flat on my face. I thought to myself, *This is crazy. I do not know what I am doing. I do not think that I can handle any more rounds in this crazy arena. I am so tired. I feel so very worn out.* I did not stay there for too long. I did get back up. I have come to realized that there is no such thing as failing with God. God never gave me an F. Thankfully, I have not flunked out in His schooling. He was not that type of teacher. I think He would give me all A's for the first time in my life. I got to keep doing things over until I got them right, until I learned and passed the class. It has been one test after another. But thankfully, I am going places. I am not just sitting here, taking up space.

I left the decision about the ten thousand dollars up to Larry. He wanted to sow it, and so we did. I cannot honestly say that I knew that was God telling us to do that. I did not know. I was still learning to recognize Him and His voice. It sounded like a good thing. It felt like a good thing to do. I had heard stories about others who had done these sorts of things and had seen desirable results. But I cannot say that I knew it was God. I have no doubt in my mind that God sometimes does ask people to sow ten thousand dollars and much more than that. I just know He does. But there is a time and a place for these things.

I have heard of some very stupid things happening. And I had a part in it all too. Putting money on a credit card that you cannot pay off—even if it's for a Christian cause—is a stupid thing. I did it, and I don't plan on ever doing it again. Not paying your taxes on time because you are sowing giant seeds into the kingdom is stupid. I did it. And I received very undesirable consequences as a result. All of the interest could have been extra money going for a greater cause. God is a God of order. He wants us to pay our bills and be responsible. I do not want to have to rely on Him for one miracle after another to get me out from a financial mess—all because I gave away my money. Well, I sowed it. I am very careful about what I allow myself to listen to now. I do not just listen to just anything and everything that sounds good. Nor do I just pick up any book and assume everything written in it is true. I am careful about what I allow my eyes to look upon and careful about what my ears hear and listen to. God has given me wisdom. It would be foolish not to use it.

I did not understand how God could be so very present in those meetings if what was taking place was not of Him. I thought back then that a person had to perform perfectly in order to get God's attention and receive His healing. I did not understand what a real gift meant. The gifts that I was familiar with all came with strings attached. Performance was involved. I did not think that God would be so very present if something was off. I did not understand it. I was hurt by it for sure. As angry as I became, I still wasn't supposed to judge. I was very upset. I wanted to go and arrest those people and set them straight with the Holy Ghost. My flesh wanted to have its say in the matter too. I wanted something to be done. I was not the only one trampled on either. I believed a world full of people had been duped a time or two. It was not God's fault. I wanted to defend Him. I wanted to expose what was really going on. I lost the desire to attend those meetings. We were given the first-class treatment, and it was fun while it lasted. It did come at a large price.

I had not heard of spiritual abuse until after I went through it all. It would had been the perfect setup if I had gotten upset with God and lost complete trust in Him and His goodness. But God sustained me. I knew better after it was over because of Him. I got to finally see what had been at play in what many considered Christian arenas. Some of it was God. There's no doubt about that. But then man's flesh gets involved. I do not believe that the Spirit was involved in all that happened there

When people do not know the truth or the Word for themselves, they can easily be set up and duped. None of us are perfect in this flesh. The spiritual man in us has been made perfect, but we do still have this flesh pulling at us. In my case, I was warring with the flesh.

Why would people try to give money so they could get a healing? Why do that when you can just believe and receive it? You can find out what God has to say about healing and being healed and just believe Him. Just take Him at His Word. Then give from a thankful heart, not out of fear. God loves a cheerful giver anyhow. Not a fearful one. He will still love you whether you give or not. We are called to be obedient when God gives us instruction and to do what we know we are here to do. But we are also called *believers*. Parts of this Christian walk is about believing and receiving. Believe, receive, and rest. At times that is the very best faith in action!

The enemy deceived me and got me to think he was God and to follow him. He could really mess with my head and my heart. His mission was to get me to walk away from God because I was hurt, hopeless, and depressed. My mind wrestled with those feelings. I knew better. I knew God was there somewhere. Somehow He would get to me and get me out of the mess. And somehow He would heal my heart. What was so troubling to my mind was the thought of God leading me into all of this and allowing me to suffer the way that I was suffering all in hope of teaching me something. The tug-of-war was on. I felt so exhausted, trying to figure out who was who, who was speaking this, and who was speaking that. Which way do I go?

I had never been interested in playing the lottery. Nor was it something that I thought I would go out and do on a weekly basis either. I thought it was God calling me to play. It seemed so awkward at first. It did not feel right. But soon my emotions got all tangled up, and all of the so-called right people came into the picture. They all believed that this was God. It was supposedly His divine instruction to me. I'd better keep doing it until He says to stop. God will send the right people into your life. But the Devil sends people too. And those people sent by him do not even have to know who is at play. It is not like they are all out to get you. Sure, I have met at least one like that. But mostly, I dealt with other deceived Christians. I had the so-called winning numbers, and I played the exact ones over and over again for more than a year. It was one huge disappointment right after another. I quickly lost interest in the idea of winning all of the money. It did not take me long. It was one hurtful blow right after another, and it had nothing to do with the money. That was not even my main concern. I did not have to win the lotto to become an heir to His throne. I already was just that—a royal heir! It was not about the money. It was all about the assignment. My heart wanted to know God. My heart wanted to hear God for myself. My heart wanted to obey. My heart wanted to go forward and to go further.

It was so mentally disturbing. You think you are following God. You see other spiritual people who are involved, people you trust and love. They are supposed to be the one's higher in rank than you. They appear to be further along than you, or so you think. And you trust them. Every week you play the exact same numbers over and over again. They do not come through. They do not produce what was spoken to you. You question if you can hear God. Something seems very wrong, but you keep on going. You stay in the game, and you are persistent and diligent. There is a manifestation that appears to be God. The people you have put your trust in and have opened your heart to tell you it is God. They are excited with you. They pray with you. They believe with you. But then some start to think that they need the winning ticket. It was not happening with me. But I had the numbers. Or so I thought.

I still questioned the entire thing. When I was alone and quiet, something inside of me just did not feel right. Where in the world was this outward manifestation coming from? It was supposed to be God. I was following it, and I was told to follow it. After a year of that, I was fed up. I had lost interest and wanted no part in it. I had no more expectancy of really winning anymore. I was so fed up with the lotto. I came to hate playing the lottery. It was hurtful and disappointing.

The real truth did come forth. And I did get delivered from all of the deception that had been in my life—spiritual things that had attached themselves to me, generational curses that I wanted broken. I had spiritual rights, and I was rising up to take a hold of them. *Enough was enough*. I was closing the doors. I wanted all the cracks sealed shut.

"Oh, Lord, release me from this madness! This cannot be You." That became the cry of my heart. I even told Him, "Sorry if I am wrong. I am done with this game." I was no longer participating. I came to hate to lotto. I did not want any part of it. I did not want to ever hear of the lottery again. And the enemy had played me in order to try to stop me from ever getting back up and back out in my game. The Devil did not like my gift of faith. He feared it. He feared me. It was all a ploy to try to stop me. My real enemy did not want me knowing God, knowing my identity, or believing. He tried to put me in a pit of doubt and depression.

The enemy even used someone to write me a letter mocking me and my God! Pause and think of that. Your dream may really be someone else's nightmare. The letter was so disturbing because it was hurtful. Not because I had doubt and disbelief about the things of God. I cried many tears, but then I would begin to laugh in a way that I had not known before. This laughter would rise up from deep within me. Then I would descend back into the tears before I then was back to laughing. So perhaps it was my flesh doing the crying and my spirit causing the laughter. My spirit knew what this letter was suggesting. My spirit had the faith to believe God. My heart believed God. I knew and knew that God was not going to let me down. And He sure was not putting me to shame. God would come through for me like He always did and always had. It was only a matter of time. Yes, a matter of time. Faith and patience go together. My flesh hurt because of the person who has sent this letter. My flesh hurt because this person had once claimed to love me. When I came to the real truth about this individual, I knew he knew nothing about real love. I did not believe that there was any truth in this individual. I believe that truth had been rejected. There was nothing there but a life of deception. God only knows the heart. The fruit spoke for itself.

I have had this faith in me, and I just would not let go, even when I tried to kill it myself. This faith in me would just get back up and get out from the grave. It appeared to be dead in areas for a brief time. But it would spring back up. It popped back up out of the grave. I do not know of any other way to put it. It happened more times than I could count. A dream would not die. This dream was so very thrilling in the beginning, and it continued on in amazement. And when I caved into doubt, I did not remain there. Doubt would try to tell me that I was a crazy white woman. It was far too out there. I did not even know how to do my part. I did not know how to do what my heart kept coming back to. My flesh wanted no part in this. It would have preferred to run away a long time ago. This flesh of mine would have preferred to stay in a beach home for a holiday.

But not the spirit in me. That was not going to settle. That was not giving up so easily. It was willing to keep on fighting, believing, and trusting, even when the spirit in me was feeling wiped out. It got back up. The one who lifted my head and my heart would get me back up. The faith in me just simply would not let go. That bulldog faith in me lived. It was alive again. It could not be killed. No matter how bad it appeared to be, regardless of my outward appearances, there was still life in me. There was still a great life to live out. The best was yet to come! And there would be no shame about it.

A dear friend of mine once said to Larry, "Even if God tells Jennifer to get out on the interstate with a large sign in her hand and for her to march up and down the highway, she would do it"! And she was right. I would do that if God told me.

In the midst of all of that past confusion, I did not find a pot of gold in the back lawn. I realize it sounds crazy to some. It even sounds crazy in my own head. But to my heart, it sounds entirely different. There was a sound of faith. God's gold there and God's gold here are the same. Gold is gold, my friend. If He tells me to believe Him, then I will. Some say that He would not do such a thing. And those are the very ones who will never see it for themselves. God is rich. He is very rich indeed. I am more like Him than I thought. No wonder I like the things that I do.

I have been told by ordinary people as well as people who have carried great titles that they have yet to meet anyone with my kind of faith. It has inspired some. It has encouraged some. It has helped some. And I give God the glory for it all. It still amazes me. He amazes me. I was even asked to be in a place of great power. It felt overwhelming. I wanted to go. It made me feel important. If you only knew. It was like an invite of a lifetime back then. Larry said no. He had a very difficult time telling me no. But he did it. Feeling important and being important are two very different matters of the heart. Now that I have had the revelation, I can move on in the right direction.

I do believe that 2016 is my year—the year that I have been waiting for. I've had seven years of preparation. And those years were not spent off in the spa with ongoing beauty treatments either. Unusual and out-of-the-box thinking does not frighten me. I anticipate it. I expect it. My heart has taken over my mind many times. My heart just has to tell my mind to be quiet, to stop the thinking and reasoning and trying to figure things out. All of that reasoning will stop you from believing. It could stop you from believing your greatest miracle. I have come too far to turn back now. And besides, there is nothing to turn back to. That would be a miserable life to live. The only way for me is forward. I am making it to the top of my mountain. I am climbing to the top. My heart is still beating, and my heart is still believing. It is alive and well. God did get my house in order. God did heal my heart in more areas than I thought existed.

God did hold my marriage together, even during a time when I would have gladly said good riddance to Larry. And I am quite sure Larry would have said the same thing to me. We had our differences for sure. We came from opposite ends of the earth. We had very different mind-sets. And we both were very opinionated. As soon as I started really speaking my mind and heart, we clashed. It annoyed me more than I can put into words. I was not going to settle and go back to the way that I was either. I did not like that person. It was not even the real me. The real me finally came forth. And I liked her.

God had a safe place for me already planned out. He did have a plan of escape for me. I was not running from my problems. But I was headed to my safe place where I could get free from them. God knew the right Christian He had predestined for me to meet. God had prearranged the entire thing. All I had to do was obey. The enemy tried using a little offense to keep me out from that place too—the place that God had for me. I had enough spiritual sense to discern it. He was giving me wisdom. I could hear God, and I was learning.

In the midst of all of the confusion and commotion with the lottery and other people, I had to deal with a loved one disappearing. This person had left a letter that he was going to end his life. I never knew what wailing before the Lord was until this happened. I could not imagine a suicide. I could not imagine what it would be like living out the remainder of your time here, dealing with something like this. It's one thing when a person takes another person's life and when accidents happen. It is all awful. But when people are so down and low and goes as far as to end their lives to escape the pain, that is another matter altogether. I have felt that type of pain. I just could not do what this person had set out to do. God was with me through the fight for my life. There was no suicide. It was emotionally draining though, especially on top of all that had already happened. It seemed like everything was falling apart.

I did not feel like praying another prayer. I had no song left in me to sing. I felt like I was out of breath. I did not want to get out of my bed. I would have rather just stayed right there and pulled my fluffy duvet cover over me. I felt done. My fire did not feel like it could flame again. I did not know what to do. If you cannot turn to God, then who can you run to? No man or woman was going to fix this. God could use one or the other or both. But I had to make sure that I got to the right place at the right time regardless of how I felt.

God called me out again. It was time to move and to just go. I wanted to get out from that house. I had no interest in it. I did not even like it anymore. It meant nothing to me. I was more than ready to leave. I did not care about losing the house. I was happy. I did not care about the money. Many would considered it a huge loss. I flat out did not care. Larry, on the other hand, was not so thrilled about it. For some reason, God would always deal with me when He wanted us to move out! It was not comfortable facing Larry with all that came to me. But it was very good training ground and preparation for me.

You could not have paid me to stay there in that house. I was done with that place. The house went to foreclosure. The business was barely staying afloat. We were out running all over the place, chasing after what we thought was God. There was no time to look after the business. It was hanging on by a single thread. It may have sunk, but it was not destroyed. I had spent two years locked up in my house, searching for ways to know God. I did leave the house. But it was nothing like before. I did what I had to do. I went where I needed to go and could not seem to wait to get back home. I was a desperate white woman. I wanted more. And I was determined that if anyone could have more, it was going to be me!

I had my own prayer closet, and that was where I lived most of the time. I would hear the little feet of my children go by as they looked for me. I know that my children did not understand me. And at times they may still not always get me. Many people have not understood me and my ways. Many thought I went overboard. Perhaps I did. I wanted to walk on the water! I dove right on in and was going to the very bottom before I would ever come back up to the surface and make it to the top.

But my children did not know that what I was doing was not just about me. It was also for them. I did not want them repeating the mistakes of my old life. I wanted far better for them. I had big dreams for them. And it was truly for them. I didn't want to try to live my life through their success either. I had my own life to live, and I was living it. I was blazing my own trail and fighting not only for my future but for theirs too. I did not want them to have to fight the battles that I had. I wanted to pave the way and take my position in Christ. I believed that I was the one that God had chosen in my family to rise up. I wanted to make a difference.

God moved us off to a new location still in Georgia. It was a new place, and we had a fresh start. God had already arranged for the healing of my heart. The Lord did lead me by the still waters. There were very still waters inside of me. God had been speaking to me. He was telling me that I did not know who I was in Him, that I needed to rest in Him! I was desperate to understand what He meant. So many times I believe I heard that soft, refreshing voice time and time again, telling me to rest and to be still.

I had prayed and prayed and prayed. I had made so many heartfelt confessions over and over again. I had rebuked that Devil more times than I could count. I even got to cast him out of a person. I sang my songs. I prayed and fasted plenty of times, not usually getting the results that I wanted. I had given out everything there was to give out. I felt empty and just exhausted. Many moments I needed to remember to breathe. My breath felt as if it had gone out of me. I had many questions without answers. There were days and nights of temptations, when I would just hear a voice telling me give up. This was not what I asked for. This was not what I thought I had signed up for. I still needed to discover that I could be right even though I did not feel right. I could still be strong even though I was so very weak.

Never in my life did I think that I would need to fight in the way I had chosen to fight for my children. And I was in real faith with what I was up against—the Devil himself. My faith was alive and real and it worked. I did get the results that I believed I would. I did not give up and give into defeat. *No way!* Not when it came to my kids. I fought and fought and fought some more. I did not yield to doubt and unbelief. And I fought against the fear—fear that would not to leave me alone. Evil had been at play. Deception and lies literally wore me out. Even the spirit inside of me was burned out. It was an absolute miracle that I looked the way that I looked. I still looked younger than I actually was. God has preserved me. His power has been far better than any expensive face cream that I have applied to my face. "I was being enlightened with the Light of the Living. My flesh was being restored. God had promised that it would become fresher and more tender than a child's; that He would return me to the days of my youth" (see Job 33:25 AB). Well, I had no desire to get back to my youth. I believed for something better. I do get compliments on my skin on a regular basis. To God be the glory! People have taken notice—that is for sure. It is pretty smooth. I must say that I do enjoy

God was ready to teach me what He meant by being still. It was not about me continually confessing His Word over and over. Nor was it about me rebuking that Devil over and over. I did not feel like there was any prayer left in me. God was calling me to be still and to rest. Good things are not always God things. To me, a God thing is when you are led by Him to do what He is saying. It is obedience. That is what this entire learning lesson has been about—knowing Him and knowing how to follow Him. Why? Because I trust Him. I choose to trust Him. I do believe that He has my very best interest at heart. I do believe that He loves me and has great plans for me. I do believe that there is still much He has to say about me, Jennifer. I do not believe that my time is over. I am going to see what He has shown me on the inside of my heart. I will see it happen.

God has known what I needed and when I needed it for every season. It was my part, my job to listen to Him, to follow Him. It was time to be *quiet* and to sit still. I did not know that. But I learned. Actually doing what God is saying and doing what we think we are supposed to do are sometimes at opposites ends of the field. I do not have all of the answers, but I do have the one who does. And that is all that matters.

During that time something happened that if it had not been for the Lord in my life I would had gone totally AWOL onto a person. Do not mess with my child. The angry white woman rises again! It hurt and stung me so badly that all I could do was laugh in the Holy Ghost. I learned earlier on in another previous battle how to fight and win. I won that war. Praise the Lord! He won it through me because I cooperated with Him. I knew better than to give into the fear and to lose hope. I just began to laugh and to laugh and laugh out loud. Hallelujah! That annoyed the Devil too. What can he do to a person like that? I just laughed. I believed that the outcome would turn out far differently than what was taking place. The Devil tried to break my heart again. And even though he got to it, I laughed anyway. I trusted in and was confident in my Lord. So I laughed some more.

Sitting in one of those conferences, I will not ever forget that time. I sat there in my seat at the very end of the aisle. I was close enough to make eye contact with the preacher. He implied that to know God and to be called of God, it could perhaps cost you your life. I took that to heart. I sat there in fear. I said to God, "I will give You whatever You want or require of me. *But please do not take my coffee!*" I thought that since I enjoyed my coffee as much as I did, it might be taken from me. Perhaps it was an idol to me just like the handbag, just like the expensive clothes and shoes. Since I liked all of those things so much, maybe God would ask me to let it all go in His name. Or so I thought. Fear tormented me. And since I liked my long beautiful hair, I cut it all off a time or two for Him. I wanted to prove that there was not anything that

I would not turn over to Him. I thought it was all required of me to be dead and alive to Him. There's religion. But it's another thing altogether to have a relationship with your maker. I had a desperate heart that was desperate to please at any cost.

Knowing him cost me everything that I can think of, including my coffee and my long hair. I purposely had the hair cut off a time or two while I was living in Georgia. I thought that perhaps I liked my hair just a little too much, that my hair could be an idol to me. Now I know that was a devilish experience. There certainly was no life and peace about it. I sacrificed not having my hair. But for what? For wrong thinking. I was duped and deceived. I did not know. So I tried. I stepped out to find out. I did eventually find out. It was not God who required me to do such foolishness either. I so wanted that hair to grow back overnight. I even asked for it. But I cannot say that I was in real faith about that request. I did not know for sure if God would really do something like that. He may have wanted to teach me a lesson. That is what some would say. He may have used this experience to transform me into someone who is more like Christ. If I hadn't been ignorant, then I would have known that I was already like Him.

Some people from my past made such a deal about all of my faults and the things that they thought were wrong about me. They were called Christian people. They said that they were anyway. I do not honestly know their hearts. God does. I am not going to be their judge like they were mine. I wound up trying to prove to myself that they were all so very wrong about me. So regardless of all of my losses, I did gain quite much after all. I got my own answers about who I really was. And what I really stood for. As well as what was most important to me. I was able to see my own heart and what really mattered. God got to see it too. He watched and witnessed the entire ordeal.

Faith is the assurance (the confirmation) of the things we hope for. It is the proof of things we do not see and the conviction of their reality. Faith perceives what is not revealed to the senses (Hebrews 11:1

AMP). The heroes of faith are all in the Bible. And we learn that without faith, it is impossible to please God. He likes faith. He created faith. He responds to faith. I cannot say that I had full assurance in some of the things I asked for. That was another entire lesson. I thought at the time I was in faith, but I was not. I had too many uncertainties, too many questions that needed answers. I was not going to settle for some sort of sermon or traditional teaching. I look back at the foolishness and ignorance. I was able to see the innocence in me. I had a heart to please others. I wanted to please. I wanted God to be pleased with me. I needed to use my great faith and just believe that He already was.

Jesus came and did what I was not able to do. I do believe that He felt forsaken as he hanged there all beat up on that cross. I can only imagine the people standing there and scoffing as He endured for you and me. They all wondered, *Where is Your God now?* God knew what was going on the entire time. Even though it appeared that Jesus had been forsaken, He was not. God raised Him from that grave of death on the third day! Jesus got up! Hallelujah! He is the Messiah. He came and did what He had promised. He did go all the way for me and for you. I was not qualified to do what Jesus did. Nor would I want to. The price has been paid for my freedom. I needed to really get that straightened out.

It seems to me that every time I set out to make a change in my life, I wanted the support of another. I wanted approval to know that it was okay, that I was okay. I wanted someone to tell me that it was the right thing for me to do. Some things were very certain to me. No doubt about it. Other things I did struggle with. I wanted to make sure that I was hearing right, that it was really God, and that God was okay with the change that I desired to have for myself. I needed to listen to Him with my heart and not rely on other people in order for Him to take me where He wanted me to go. That's why I needed a personal relationship with Him. So too, there will be people who can help you in the process of getting to know the real Him.

The dreams of my heart have not been little. They have not all been petty things. It has been a fight of a lifetime to keep them, not to drop them and to walk away. I did try that a time or two. Then I would find myself crawling back to God with a humbled heart. And as I grew up in Him, I was able to finally run to Him. Holding on to all inside of me has not been easy, for doubt wants to creep in. Now that I got past the "Who do you think you are, and how do you think God could ever use you?" It is "What do you even want to do all of that for?" Who said that I did? This flesh of mine has wanted to bail more times than I can count. Much is at stake. If I were to walk away from the dream, then where would I go? What do I have to believe other than the fact that I am saved and that I am going to heaven when I die? I would not have much to go back to. It would be such a boring life after all that I had endured. I know too much now. In fact, to walk away from it frightens me. I would miss out on the greatest blessing other than having Jesus as my Lord and Savior. I would miss my purpose.

I hate second-guessing myself. It is tormenting when you think you have made your final decision only to find yourself pulled back into reasoning and out from your place of peace. I hate it. I am not so headstrong that I will not listen to reason from another. I have listened to it plenty of times. But I learned that reasoning has nothing to do with faith or a believing heart. I am not the type to be talked out from something that I truly believe, something that I know God has spoken to my heart. I will fight for truth. I will stand and fight for what I believe in. This whole process of being taught how to be led of the Spirit has not been easy. That has been my heart's desire—to know the real Him and to know when the real Him is speaking to me. I want to know what He is saying and what He is asking me to do. And there has been an entire army out there trying to stop me, trying to hold me back. They disguise themselves as something they are not, and they try to feed me one lie after another. They are counterfeit, all in hope of leading me astray. But here comes the marvelous light. He shines again and again and again!

Hallelujah! I have seen the light. And I do believe that I know what I am talking about. There is no questioning, no reasoning, no wondering about it. I have His love. Thank You, Jesus!

A person can give it all away and still not be right with God. Just because you walk away from all you like and enjoy or think you enjoy, that does not make you right. People can still covet and still have the love of money even though they do not have any. There is nothing wrong with having lots of money, and there's nothing wrong with possessing nice stuff. People can still have wrong attitudes whether they possess stuff and money. Now here is a truth to stop and examine. The love of money is what is wrong. We are called to worship God, not money. We as believers are called to trust God with providing for us and our needs. I am learning that God is a God of great provision. He sure does know how to provide. He is my Jehovah-Jireh.

This life of mine has been one of learning. Much stepping out and finding out has taken place. I have had my share of tears and heartbreak too. But then I have had my share of healing. I've been knocked down, but God causes me to rise back up and to ride again. Honestly, I have not been back on a horse ever since I was thrown off of one. I'm not kidding. I got bucked off riding as a young teen, and I have not ridden since. But this is a different type of riding. The type of riding I am talking about is like a riding of the Spirit to me. The more and more that I become acquainted with Him, the less I am knocked down. I can just flow in the Spirit of God regardless of the situation and the circumstances. Tests and trials will come. But now I know that I do not have to be tossed and thrown off by them. I can still live on top of the mountain. I can be happy regardless of what comes my way.

I would step out to begin one particular process, but then I would find myself all beat up from it. I would get halfway through it and feel defeated and give into doubt. I would think that I was crazy for ever trying in the first place. I would think that it was never going to turn out right. I would lose hope and give up. It was very frustrating. I truly wanted a support system, one that would see what I saw and help me by encouraging me to stay with it regardless of how bad it temporarily looked. That support system could tell me that it would eventually get to the way that I wanted, the way that I envision it. It would work out for me. It would. I just needed to hold on and keep at it until the desired results came about. I knew what I wanted. I knew what I saw. I knew what I liked. But not all could see it. Not all could visualize it. Not all agreed with me. That caused me to second-guess myself. It caused confusion. It caused doubt. But only because I allowed it for a time.

The support system that I carried with me was more than enough for me. The Holy Ghost was trying to help me. But it was going to require my cooperation. He knew where I desired to go. And He was perfectly capable of taking me there. I had trust issues. I wanted to make sure I was trusting in the right person, not some counterfeit. It was not all nice and easy going through this process either.

My papa used to say that so many give up too soon and right before their biggest breakthroughs. Oh, Lord, help me. Do not let that be me. I now see the picture painted out perfectly right before my eyes.

The very thing that I did with my hair, I have done with parts of my dream. I was up in the faith only to find myself pulled back down. It is so far out there and not humanly possible—at least not for me. It would take a massive miracle. It would take the hand of God. My God. Why have I, Jennifer, had such a difficult time believing Him? I felt tossed back and forth. Reasoning is not faith. It has nothing to do with the life of faith. I had been sucker-punched long enough. I do believe that now is the time for me to hang onto my dream like never before and refuse to doubt in any sort of way. I have hung onto real faith in certain areas. I got the results that I believed and fought for too. It worked out just perfectly great. Other areas of faith have needed some growth. I needed some strength training. I saw the vision. There was no doubt about it. I have needed to majorly prepare to really believe and to keep believing. The enemy has tried time and time again to destroy me and my big faith. It has been quite the battle. But it has gotten much easier, not because this enemy gives up and goes away for good but because I have learned how to fight the good fight of faith.

My hair fell out. It died. It could not take any more going back and forth. It had enough. It held on for as long as it could last, and then it broke. It all broke off, and out it came, thankfully not from the roots. But I did end up with a very short hair. It looked just like a man's haircut. It was not what I wanted. Never in my life did I dream of having my hair this way. It suits some, but it was not me. I hate what has happened to me—the undesirable things. But I am glad in a way. I am happy that I did not allow fear to hold me back and prevent me from trying. I went for what I have wanted.

I have not enjoyed waking up some mornings and staring at rooster hair in the mirror either. I am not used to this. I do prefer my long, luxurious hair. I want to wake up with it all in place. That is quite nice. What I now currently see is not what I am stuck with. I am well able to see past my set of circumstances. I am no longer confused. I am going somewhere. I do see and see quite well. There is no problem with my eyesight. This is going to work out right for me. Once I get something in my heart, I have this fighting faith about it. I am not going to let it drop. Or I just won't leave it alone. It causes me to rise up and to believe again. I have heard it said that we should wait and hear God before we move out. Well, if I would had done that starting out, then I would still most likely be waiting. I did not know if I heard Him correctly in the very beginning. I second-guessed myself because of the confusions from my past. My past seemed to be causing me very much trouble in trusting myself and God and all that He had arranged for me.

The only way that I was going to know for sure was to get up and try. That was the only way for me. I had to know. I was not willing to live with what-if questions. I tried many things that I thought I was to supposed do. Many of them came from God. Plenty did not. So I have learned both ways. There have been consequences for my actions.

I have been through both good and bad times. And now I know. I can now look back and see the times that God by His Spirit tried to stop me. But like a wild horse, I took off running anyway. I did not know. One can feel so strongly about a thing, but that does not mean that it is God. Or the timing or how you must go about achieving a goal may not be what you think.

I am so very thankful that God has not left me alone in some of those most undesirable set of circumstances. He was with me and did not walk out on me. He has provided me an escape when need be. Of course, people who wait and know that they know they have heard God stay protected. Most likely, they do not have a hard set of circumstances to endure by waiting until they know for sure. Consequences arose from not waiting and not really knowing. I have had a lifetime of them. I was not a fan of reading the instructions. I just set out on my course. I was given just enough information to get me started. It was rather exciting. I did not think that I would have ever done such a thing either. Never in my wildest dreams did I think that I would bleach my own head of hair, let alone cut all the dead stuff off. Larry was right. My bathroom had turned into my science laboratory, and I came out looking rather mad a few times or two. Larry's little warrior had turned into a mad scientist! It was rather thrilling, watching the process of the black transforming into the lighter shades on top of my head. I was thrilled that I had the ability to do it myself without any training. I just did it.

A few years ago, I would have panicked. As much as I hated that, it happened, and I still was able to hold myself together. I had the internal stability that I needed. Obviously, much growth has taken place. I hate that I lost my hair, but it was worth it. I learned a valuable lesson. And I got to be me. I did what I had wanted to do for a very long time. I got past listening to what others wanted or thought I should do.

I know who I am and to whom I belong. That makes all the difference in the world to me. I am still God's little princess with or without the hair. But I do thank the Lord for hair extensions! It has helped in the process. I have not given up on God, for He never gave up on me. He has been with me through it all. He did not turn His back on me. My faith has grown. As long as I stay on track with my heart's belief, then I have life, and I have much peace. I have joy for what is to come. When the enemy comes in to pounce on me, then doubt and unbelief try to interfere with all that I believe. Those are the times that have caused me to feel down. So what does one like that do? Fight back? Fight the good fight of faith? That is not the time to start questioning and reasoning all that you believe. That is the time to hang on to that dream and not let it die. There is a time for everything. When the dream thief comes, do not give him what is rightfully yours. This has required more work than I thought. If he has stolen your dream, then take it back! I took the harder course after all. Believing is not easy when you don't really believe. You want to believe. You desire to believe for all that your heart yearns for. But you question it. You wonder if it is real. You try to reason it out with your head, and it only makes it worse. There is no way that head knowledge will bring about the answer you desire. It is not about the head. It is all about the heart. My heart. Your heart. What's in your heart is what matters, and it matters more than some know.

Free to Be Me

"What do I like?" I was free to finally ask myself that question. And I was free to answer it honestly without hesitation. I had broken free of the unspoken rules from my past. The chains were gone, and I was free. I was no longer afraid that I might answer the question all wrong. There was not a right or wrong answer about it. *What are my likes? What are my dislikes?* Now I know. Asking myself those two things had nothing to do with what other people wanted me to be like. What does this person or group of people want me to like or not like? What does God want me to like? I got free from people's approval. I had God's approval. It had been there ever since I became His child. I did not know. It was all part of getting to know Him. I was no longer tormented in trying to please people. That was not what I have been called to. That really was a curse. That is another trap for more rejection, especially if you did not want to do what is required of you. If you allow people to tell you who you are when they do not even know who they are, then you are in for one ride of your lifetime, and it's not an enjoyable experience either.

I love people. I even enjoy people now. I like to bless people. I like to help people. I like to put a smile on another's face. I want to build people up, not tear them down. I am concerned about others that God has put on my path. I have a heart for people. What more can I say? I am no longer afraid of people. Not all people like me, but plenty do.

God has given me much favor. He has truly blessed me. And when rejection comes, it will not cripple me. I have overcome with the Lord. Praise God!

I did not know who I was, for I was too caught up in trying to be what the people around me wanted me to be. In order for me to feel loved or accepted, I had to perform right. It felt as if love was withheld if I did not. Or I would see expressions of disapproval or hear disapproval in voices. Rejection was at play. I had come to a place where I could be honest and true to myself. I was breaking free from that old victim mentality. I was not powerless. I was not defeated. I certainly wasn't going to live the rest of my life as some sort of victim. That was not my case. I was a special case. I was determined to be free. No more putting up with lies. And no more clucking around in the chicken coop with a bunch of chickens that were afraid of telling the truth. I was going to fly like the eagle.

I landed in a safe place with a safe person, one whom God had handpicked and chosen to help get me through the process of becoming. I was ready to become all I had once dreamed I could be. I let go of the false humility that I carried around. I was no longer the wretched sinner. Just because someone wrote a song that is often sung in some churches, that does not even mean all of the lyrics and words are correct. It may sound right. It may even feel right, but that does not mean that it is true. I am not some wretched sinner. I will tell you what I am. I can now, for I have truly found *my voice. I am redeemed.* I have been redeemed by the blood of the Lamb. I have been made perfect in His sight, all thanks to Jesus. I keep my eyes focused and planted on Christ, and that tells me who I am. I am with Him. Praise God!

I like the song by Diana Ross, "I'm Coming Out." That is my song as far as I am concerned. I am no longer afraid. I got free from my shell. This flesh just has to go where the Spirit in me is leading. I am a new creature in Christ.

Jesus reigns supreme inside of my heart. God did hear my petition to

Him, and I did find favor in His sight. He granted me my heart's desire. My God did not withhold the request from my lips. My King, Jesus Himself, did send blessings of good things and people to meet me. I feel now as if He has set a crown of pure gold on my head. I asked for life from Him, and He gave it to me. My glory is great because of Your aid, oh Lord, and Your splendor and majesty You seem to enjoy bestowing these gift on me. You make me to be blessed and a blessing forever. You make me exceedingly glad with the joy of Your continual presence. I trust and rely on You, Lord, and through the mercy and steadfast love of my most high God, *I will never be moved* (see Psalm 21:2–7 AB).

Regardless of the deceit that was at play, God's truth prevailed and came through for me. He is faithful. And His Word is true. God touched me. He removed all of the blue and got me out from the glue. I am not stuck anymore. I am not afraid of that Devil. He has tried to scare me long enough. I am not saying that I never feel fear. But I am not stuck in it. And I don't bow down to it or run from it. I face it head on. Just like a warrior would. The Lord is a warrior; the Lord is His name (see Exodus 15:3). And so am I! *Charge!* God knows where He will take me from here. Hallelujah!

I have become a lady at rest. Resting on His promises does not mean I am floating around in the clouds. That is not the type of rest I am referring to. The greatest part of the dream was just that. Once I got to know Him, then I got to know me. I did get a new birth. And I had been filled. I did discover that I did have legal rights after all. My enemy did not want me finding out about what I had actually received. He sure did not want me knowing about my new rights. And he most definitely did not want me exercising my truth.

I am a citizen of heaven, and I do have spiritual rights after all. I come from true royalty. He is just that, and so am I. I am suited up and dressed to kill. I fight lies. That is my new sport. In the game of tennis, I learned to keep my eyes planted on the ball. I don't look off at the fence or where I want to hit the ball. Keeping my eyes on the ball was not as easy as one may think. There were plenty of distractions going on around me and inside of me. It was a discipline that I had to learn and to develop. Now the same is true in the spiritual world. I needed to keep my eyes on Jesus. I knew what He had already done for me. So when those balls come a flying at me, I know how to hit them. I know how to aim and to fire. Many times I say, "Oh no, you do not. You are not coming in here. You are not about to do that to me. *Get out intruders!* Now I know better."

I overcame struggles by the blood of the Lamb and by the Word of my testimony (see Revelation 12:11). I do not understand that Devil. I cannot even begin to comprehend his fierce anger and hatred. It has gotten far worse for him because he knows his time is running short. I do not understand him, because I am nothing like him. I am of God. I have God's nature operating in me. I am fully aware of that now. I have true peace. I know where I am going! I know who I am. I know to whom I belong. I know what I am not. I have nothing to prove. My God has already done that for me. I am so very thankful for rest.

I laugh so hard at times when I think about the lady in the department store. It happened in Georgia. A little fashion show took place with us. We got to talking. Something I said set off something inside of her. She turned and looked at me and said, "You cannot go down there like that! Those women will eat you alive! You have to get yourself a new walk." So this woman held up the dress that I was holding in the department. She placed it right in front of her and began to strut across the floor. She said to me, "You have to walk like this!" Head up, shoulders back, and a face full of confidence. That was God confidence. She rises again! Let Your fire in me shine forth like never before, dear Lord. You are my Lord, my life, the true lover of my soul. My heart got it. My heart got You.

I have been told that I have not missed any steps on my journey. My only regret would be that I cannot honestly say that I have enjoyed all of it, even though I have made it. And I will continue to make it. I do feel so bound by the Holy Spirit. To me, that is a very good thing. I truly am coming to the place more and more where I can be like Paul of the Bible and say, "None of these things move me" (see Acts 20:24 AMP). And truly mean it. I have said those words many times only to find myself caught up in some sort of whirlwind, temporarily blown off course. The storms always passed. I have learned how to dance in the rain with deep inner joy inside of my heart. Now there is a book right there. I am not crazy. I have found my truth. I have found the answers that I have been so desperate for. Others who do not have what I have may think I went crazy. Oh, well. I am definitely not moved by that. I had to overcome that, or I would not have ever stepped into the life that God had set up for me. And I am so glad that I did step in. All it took was one single step to follow Him.

We got to move again. We finally left Georgia. It was never our plan to stay. Thankfully, it wasn't God's plan either. I enjoy the warmth and the sunshine. I enjoyed the city life while I was there. It was a great experience, and a lot of learning took place. I have learned, and I am committed in further learning. I enjoy spiritual growth. Seasons will come, and they will go. Fall was my favorite. Summer did not feel like summer there. Lakes were not my thing. I will take the ocean seashore and the warm sandy beaches any day over red clay. I did not care for those cold, rainy days with dead trees all around. Dried-up grass was not so pretty to me. I like living things and lots of green with pretty blue skies and white puffy clouds. I like to hear the birds chirping and singing. I enjoy watching the white seagulls with the wind blowing through my hair. I do like the wind. I do find some of those pelicans pretty cute. I get a kick out of locating alligators that are sunbathing. I have a good eye for them. Just knowing that the beach is right here is very satisfying to me. I have always been fascinated with the ocean. I enjoy peace. I appreciate peace. I have become addicted to peace. I did not grow up in an atmosphere of peace. I knew nothing about it. I did not have any idea about how to obtain it. But now that I do, I will fight to keep it. I will pursue it and go after it. There is just something about this ocean that puts a smile on my face. I find staring out at it peaceful. I also enjoy waking up to the sound of running water. I like large overflowing fountains. I like the palm trees, especially when they are lined up across from each other down a driveway. I have an appreciation for beauty and beautiful things. I like pretty. I like new. I really like new. I love my family and laughing with them. I now love to laugh. I have found much to laugh about. I enjoy writing, for it comes to me so very easily. It feels natural. I love to tell the truth. I desire to help others. I desire to help others know who I have come to know— the lover of my soul, Jesus. There is such intimacy in knowing Him. I want others to have that close relationship with Him. I want others to be touched and healed by Him. That is one of my greatest desires—to release what I have been given.

I love my dog, my little Chihuahua, Romeo. I have heard some say that we are not supposed to say that we love any particular thing, that we are to love God and love people only. And I do. God knows my heart, but I do love my dog too. He is like a little human to me. I love how the Lord calls me to Himself, how He touches the innermost parts of my heart. There is nobody else like Him. I love Him and how He awakens me. I yearn for Him in the longings of my soul. I wait for Him in great expectancy. He has never left me disappointed. His love touches me like no other. He moves me like no other.

I love that He has given me my own voice and that He has removed the fear so that I will use it. I love that He loved me enough to come for me and to die for me. Oh, yes, He found me too. And now I refuse to ever let go. I am not letting go. I am holding on. I am holding on like never before. I am holding on to Him and holding on to all that He has put in my heart. I refuse to let go. I am going to do all that He has shown me. I believe. I am going to see it happen with my physical eyes. All are going to see. I believe it. I have come too far to give up now. How foolish that would be. I have this faith that will not leave me alone. It keeps speaking to this heart of mine. Oh, how I love Him. I do love Him, for He first loved me. His name is so great to me. That is why I cannot stand it when people misuse it. I hate it. I suppose I did go overboard. I am glad that I did too. I'd never want to get back on the boat that I was once on. I dove in. I did not care who was watching or what anyone else thought. I was fed up with what some of those other people had to say. I had sat back quietly long enough. listening and observing. I am willing to follow—not people but my maker. I love that I can hear Him for myself. I now know that I can.

Rejection hurts. But once I get passed the sting of it, I can laugh. I laugh with real joy. I know who I am, and I know to whom I belong. I know where I come from. And I do know where I am going. I have been rejected for being honest and real. I like truth. I prefer truth. I hate lies. I choose to fight them. Even though I had witnesses in my life, God was the greatest one of all. He did not bail on me and then run away from the crime scene. He was there. He saw the whole thing. Even though my case did not go before a court of law, it did go before God's throne. God is a God of justice. He did not forget about the incident. He did not pretend that it never happened. He did not tell me that I was wrong. One of the greatest blessings that God has bestowed on me was the journey that showed me that I was right. I do believe it. I would be crazy not to.

Oh God, You healed the broken, bleeding heart. You bound up my wounds and gave me so much beauty. You have given plentiful joy for all of the mourning. A garment of powerful praise instead of those brick loads of heaviness. And dear God, I so thank You for doubling the piles of honor in exchange for the double amounts of shame (see Isaiah 61:1–3 AB). Hallelujah! Thank You, Lord. You helped me to find my way! What would have become of me had I not believed in the goodness of God in the land of the living?

My chains are gone. I've been set free. God, my Savior, has ransomed me. Like a flood, His mercy reigns. Amazing love and amazing grace.

If you desire to have this *unending, unfailing love,* if you desire to have Jesus come into your heart to *rescue* you from a life that only leads to death and destruction, then this prayer is for you.

Oh Father, oh God of heaven, I choose and I desire to believe in You. I do choose to believe in Your Son, Jesus. You did send Jesus here for me, and I believe that He rose from the dead. I acknowledge and confess Him to be my Lord and my personal Savior. Thank You, Jesus, for the cross and all that it means for me. By the blood of Jesus, I am forgiven. At this very moment, I receive You, Jesus, to come into my heart and to live inside of my heart by Your Holy Spirit. I receive You, Lord, as my entire life source, to be found and summed up all in You. Along with all that You offer and supply me. I no longer want to settle for anything. I want to receive this very moment all that You have to offer and to give me. I confess my sins now before Your throne of mercy and grace. I receive my forgiveness right now and believe that my name is now written in the Lamb's Book of Life. When I leave this place, I am coming home to live in heaven with You Jesus, my Lord. I receive this gift by faith. Touch me, Lord. Heal me, Lord. Heal my past and present wounds. Help me to forgive and to release and to bless the people who have wronged me. Your love, mercy, and grace will take over my life, my heart. By faith, the hurts and wrongs of my past are now over. Now my life truly begins. I have a new life this instant. Thank you for freeing me. You, Jesus, already paid the penalty for all of my past, present, and future sins as well as the ones done to me. Thank You for Your constant blood flow. I receive You as my healer. Come and heal me now. Baptize me with Your Holy Spirit. Fill me, Lord, with Your Holy Spirit, and give me my heavenly prayer language. Help me on this new journey of following You, hearing You, loving You, worshipping only You. I do worship You, Lord, and thank You for this new life of mine. Show me my own purpose. Show me my place. Lead me to the right church family. Lead me in safe relationships. Teach me Your ways. Teach me Your love. Teach me Your truth. Deliver me from the pits of destructive ways. Deliver me now, Jesus, from dysfunction. Deliver me from all bondage, and remove the chains of my past. In Jesus's name, amen and amen! So be it … done. Hallelujah! Glory be to God!

Printed in the United States
By Bookmasters